THE
1995 ANNUAL:
Volume 1
Training

(The Twenty-Fourth Annual)

Edited by

J. William Pfeiffer, Ph.D., J.D.

Amsterdam • Johannesburg • London
San Diego • Sydney • Toronto

PREFACE

One key to the success of the *Annual* has been its ability to meet the needs of human resource development (HRD) practitioners by providing materials of immediate, practical use. The contents of each *Annual* focus on increasing a reader's professional competence and, therefore, his or her impact on the field of HRD.

This year we have doubled our efforts to meet the needs of our readers. Beginning with 1995, Pfeiffer & Company will publish two *Annuals* each year. Volume 1 will be focused on training, and Volume 2 will be focused on consulting. For the purposes of the *Annuals,* we are considering training to be that which has an impact on individuals and consulting to be that which has an impact on organizations.

Our belief is that our readers will need and use both volumes. The decision to divide the material into training and consulting was made to make it easier for the reader to find the most appropriate materials most efficiently. Obviously, it is difficult in some cases to place materials strictly in one category or another, so there will be some overlap in what the two volumes cover.

The 1995 Annual: Volume 1, Training is the twenty-fourth volume in our *Annual* series; its contents reflect our intention to continue to publish materials that help our readers to stay on the cutting edge of the field. In keeping with this objective, users may duplicate and modify materials from the *Annuals* for educational and training purposes, as long as each copy includes the credit statement that is printed on the copyright page of the particular volume. However, reproducing Pfeiffer & Company materials in publications for sale or for large-scale distribution (more than one hundred copies in twelve months) requires *prior written permission.* Also, reproduction of material that is copyrighted by some source other than Pfeiffer & Company (as indicated in a footnote) requires written permission from the designated copyright holder.

For the *Annual* series, we are interested in receiving presentation and discussion resources (articles that include theory along with practical application); inventories, questionnaires, and surveys (paper-and-pencil inventories, rating scales, and other response tools); and experiential learning activities (group learning designs based on the five stages of the experiential learning cycle: experiencing, publishing, processing, generalizing, and applying). Contact the Editorial Department at the San Diego office for copies of our guidelines for contributors, and send submissions to the *Annual* editor at the same address.

I want to express my appreciation to the dedicated people who produced this volume. First, I offer my genuine thanks to Beverly L. Kaye, who served as an acquisitions editor for the 1995 volumes. Her contacts and her talent are responsible for a good number of the pieces in these *Annuals*. Also, I am very grateful to Dr. Beverly Byrum-Robinson, who once again has reviewed all of our experiential learning activities. Her perspective as a facilitator and her insightful recommendations play a major role in the usefulness of these training designs. I recognize and applaud the efforts and accomplishments of our Pfeiffer & Company staff: project manager, Marian K. Prokop; graphic designer and page compositor, Judy Whalen; cover designer, Lee Ann Hubbard; and the members of our editorial staff, Arlette C. Ballew, Socorro P. Gonzalez, Dawn Kilgore, Marion Mettler, Carol Nolde, and Susan Rachmeler. Finally, as always, I extend my sincere gratitude to our authors for their generosity in sharing their professional ideas, materials, and techniques so that other HRD practitioners may benefit.

J. William Pfeiffer
San Diego, California
January, 1995

About Pfeiffer & Company

Pfeiffer & Company is engaged in human resource development (HRD) and business book publishing. The organization has earned an international reputation as the leading source of practical publications that are immediately useful to today's facilitators, trainers, consultants, and managers. A distinct advantage of these publications is that they are designed by practicing professionals who are continually experimenting with new techniques. Thus, readers benefit from the fresh but thoughtful approach that underlies Pfeiffer & Company's experientially based materials, resources, books, workbooks, instruments, and tape-assisted learning programs. These materials are designed for the HRD practitioner who wants access to a broad range of training and intervention technologies as well as background in the field.

The wide audience that Pfeiffer & Company serves includes training and development professionals, internal and external consultants, managers and supervisors, team leaders, and those in the helping professions. For its clients and customers, Pfeiffer & Company offers a practical approach aimed at increasing people's effectiveness on an individual, group, and organizational basis.

CONTENTS

*See Experiential Learning Categories, p. 5, for an explanation of the numbering system.

PRESENTATION AND DISCUSSION RESOURCES

General Introduction
to the 1995 Annual

The 1995 Annual: Volume 1, Training is the twenty-fourth volume in the *Annual* series. The series is a collection of practical and useful materials for human resource development (HRD) practitioners—materials written by and for professionals. As such, the series continues to provide a publication outlet for HRD professionals who wish to share their experiences, their viewpoints, and their procedures with their colleagues.

Each *Annual* has three main sections: twelve experiential learning activities; three inventories, questionnaires, and surveys; and a series of presentation and discussion resources. Each of the pieces is classified in one of the following categories: Individual Development, Communication, Problem Solving, Groups, Teams, Consulting, Facilitating, and Leadership. Within each category, pieces are further classified into logical subcategories, which are explained in the introductions to the three sections.

Materials are selected for the *Annuals* based on the quality of their ideas, their applicability to real-world concerns, their relevance to current HRD issues, their clarity of presentation, and their ability to add to our readers' professional development. In addition, we choose experiential learning activities that will create a high degree of enthusiasm among the participants and add enjoyment to the learning process. As in the past several years, the contents of each *Annual* span a range of subject matter, reflecting the range of interests of our readers.

A list of contributors to the *Annual* can be found at the end of the volume, including their names, affiliations, addresses, and telephone numbers. Readers will find this list of contributors useful if they wish to locate the authors of specific pieces for feedback, comments, or questions. Further information is presented in a brief biographical sketch of each contributor at the conclusion of his or her article. These elements are intended to contribute to the "networking" function that is so valuable in the field of human resource development.

Pfeiffer & Company follows the stylistic guidelines established by the American Psychological Association, particularly concerning the use and format of references. Potential contributors to our publications may wish to purchase copies of the APA's Publication Manual from Order Department,

1

American Psychological Association, P.O. Box 2710, Hyattsville, MD 20784 (202-955-7600). Pfeiffer & Company also publishes guidelines for potential authors. These guidelines, revised in 1994, are published in *The 1995 Annual: Volume 2, Consulting;* they also are available from Pfeiffer & Company's Editorial Department in San Diego, California.

The editor and the editorial staff continue to be pleased with the high quality of submitted materials. Nevertheless, just as we cannot publish every manuscript we receive, readers may find that not all of the works included in a particular *Annual* are equally useful to them. We invite comments, ideas, materials, and suggestions that will help us to make subsequent *Annuals* as useful as possible to our readers.

Introduction
to the Experiential Learning Activities Section

Experiential learning activities are infinitely varied and variable. Activities should be selected based on the participants' needs and the facilitator's competence. Many activities might accomplish similar goals and be adapted to suit the particular needs of a group. However, in order for the activity to address the needs of the participants, the facilitator must be able to assist the participants in successfully processing the data that emerge from that experience.

All experiential learning activities in this *Annual* include a description of the goals of the activity, the size of the group and/or subgroups that can be accommodated, the time required to do and *process*[1] the activity, the materials and handouts required, the physical setting, step-by-step instructions for facilitating the experiential task and discussion phases of the activity, and variations of the design that the facilitator might find useful. All of these activities are complete; the content of all handouts is provided.

The 1995 Annual: Volume 1, Training includes twelve activities, in the following categories:

Individual Development: Self-Disclosure

Adventures at Work: Experiencing Work as a Movie, by Peter R. Garber (#521, page 9)

That's Me: Getting to Know Your Team Members, by Debbie Seid (#522, page 17)

---

[1] It would be redundant to print here a caveat for the use of experiential learning activities, but HRD professionals who are not experienced in the use of this training technology are strongly urged to read the "Introduction" to the *Reference Guide to Handbooks and Annuals* (1994 Edition). This article presents the theory behind the experiential-learning cycle and explains the necessity of adequately completing each phase of the cycle to allow effective learning to occur.

Individual Development: Life/Career Planning

The Hand You're Dealt: Taking a New Perspective on Career Change, by John Powell (#523, page 23)

Communication: Building Trust

Work Dialogue: Building Team Relationships, by Judith F. Vogt and Karen L. Williams (#524, page 27)

Communication: Listening

Levels of Dialogue: Analyzing Communications in Conflict, by Gary Copeland (#525, page 45)

Problem Solving: Consensus/Synergy

The Lottery: Exploring the Impact of Values on Decision Making, by R. Glenn Ray (#526, page 53)

Problem Solving: Action Planning

Values, Visions, and Missions: Using Personal Strategic Planning, by Chuck Kormanski (#527, page 59)

Groups: How Groups Work

Let's Come to Order: Getting Down to Business, by Michele M. Moomaugh (#528, page 73)

Teams: Feedback

The Helping Hand: Supporting Teammates' Goals, by Kathleen Kreis (#529, page 87)

Teams: Conflict and Intergroup Issues

Intergroup Issues

They Said, We Said: Exploring Intergroup-Conflict Resolution, by Jason Ollander-Krane and Neil Johnson (#530, page 91)

Facilitating: Opening

Your Book Jacket: Getting Acquainted, by Bonnie Jameson (#531, page 97)

Facilitating: Skills

Seaside Towers: Designing One-to-One Training, by Lisa Mayocchi, Sharon Harvey, and Ian Croft (#532, page 101)

Other activities that address certain goals can be located by using the "Experiential Learning Activities Categories" chart that follows, or by using our comprehensive *Reference Guide to Handbooks and Annuals*. This book, which is updated regularly, indexes all of the *Annuals* and all of the *Handbooks of Structured Experiences* that we have published to date. With each revision, the *Reference Guide* becomes a complete, up-to-date, and easy-to-use resource for selecting appropriate materials from *all* of the *Annuals* and *Handbooks*.

EXPERIENTIAL LEARNING ACTIVITIES

6

Pfeiffer & Company

521: ADVENTURES AT WORK: EXPERIENCING WORK AS A MOVIE

Goals

- To enable participants to share information about themselves and their work.
- To provide the participants with a framework within which to examine and assess events in their work lives.
- To provide the participants with a framework within which to think about positive change in their work lives.

Group Size

Up to thirty participants.

Time Required

Approximately one hour and forty minutes.

Materials

- One copy of the Adventures at Work Outline for each participant.
- A pencil and a portable writing surface for each participant.

Physical Setting

Any room large enough for subgroups to work without disturbing one another. Movable chairs should be provided.

Process

1. The facilitator presents the goals of the activity and describes the format in words similar to the following:

"Pretend for a moment that your job is like an adventure movie, complete with all of the thrills and suspense usually found only at your local theater. This movie has an exciting plot filled with twists and turns. The characters in your story are unpredictable; some are unexpected sources of help and others are unexpected disappointments. You may need to resort to unconventional and innovative methods to obtain the information that you need to do your job. Certain actions will be risky and could threaten your security and well-being. At times you may feel as if you cannot survive all that is facing you. In the end, however, you manage to reach your objectives.

"If you have ever felt this way about your job and work, you are not alone! Although work and life may not always be as exciting as an action-packed adventure movie, many similarities exist. Sometimes it is helpful to look at life and work in a different way in order to gain a better perspective on where we are and where we are going. We can view our jobs as more than just tasks; we can view work as an adventure.

"A great deal of 'behind the scenes' work must be done before filming begins. An exciting script must be written that will captivate the audience's attention; a producer needs to finance the movie, and a director must ensure that everything is done correctly to tell the story effectively. Stage hands must set up each scene, wardrobes need to be selected, and film and sound crews must be in place. Marketing and advertising campaigns to promote the movie also need to be created.

"In the movies, studios and production companies take care of such duties. In your movie, you need to be the one to handle these responsibilities. It is up to you to produce and promote your own career. You have the most to gain or lose in your career, and you must create the excitement and direct the actions of others who are in your movie. You must decide what should be included in your story at work and what should be edited out. It is up to you to set the stage for what will happen in your career in the future. You must be the director and one to yell 'ACTION' to begin your movie experience."

(Five minutes.)

2. The participants are instructed to form subgroups of three or four members each. The facilitator distributes copies of the Adventures at Work Outline, pencils, and portable writing surfaces. He or she gives the following instructions:

"Complete Section 1 of the Adventures at Work Outline. When all of the members of your subgroup have completed the section, discuss your responses among yourselves. You will have twenty minutes for this section—approximately ten minutes for individual writing time and ten minutes for discussion; I will let you know when ten minutes have passed."

(Five minutes.)

3. After ten minutes, the facilitator calls time and suggests that the participants begin their discussions. After ten more minutes, the facilitator reconvenes the total group and leads a discussion based on the following questions:

   ▪ What have you learned about how you view your job?

   ▪ What ideas have you heard from your fellow participants that are applicable to your views about your job?

   (Twenty minutes.)

4. The participants are asked to resume their work and complete Section 2. Once again, the facilitator reminds the participants to spend ten minutes writing and ten minutes discussing their answers. He or she calls time after ten and twenty minutes. (Twenty minutes.)

5. The total group is reconvened and the facilitator leads a discussion of the following questions:

   ▪ How does work change with the addition of supporting characters?

   ▪ How do suspense and chase scenes affect your work? How would you like to change their effects?

   (Ten minutes.)

6. The participants are asked to resume their work and complete Section 3. Again the facilitator calls time after ten and twenty minutes. (Twenty minutes.)

7. The facilitator reconvenes the total group and leads a concluding discussion based on the following questions:

   ▪ What thoughts and feeling did you experience while describing your work in movie terms?

   ▪ What did you experience about evaluating your job situation and the forces happening in it?

   ▪ What similarities and differences did you notice about reactions to work within your subgroup? What does that tell you about the nature of work?

- As a result of this activity, what steps would you like to make to change your job situation?

(Twenty minutes.)

Variations

- Subgroups can be eliminated, and the participants can share their results with the group as a whole.

- Members of an intact work team can be asked to design action plans to address obstacles identified in the Adventures at Work Outline (e.g., adjustments to the supporting cast, ways to avoid unnecessary suspense, etc.).

- The activity can be shortened by dealing with fewer of the aspects of the movie, depending on the group's context. For example, if participants are focusing on current jobs, they could deal with the scene, supporting roles, and chase. If the participants are in career transition, their focus could be on the movie review and sequel.

Submitted by Peter R. Garber.

Peter R. Garber is manager of teamwork development at the PPG Industries Flat Glass Plant in Pittsburgh, Pennsylvania. He has been with PPG since 1980, holding various positions in human resources. Mr. Garber has developed training programs in the areas of safety, quality improvement, and teamwork and has published articles on these topics. Additionally, he wrote a book entitled Coaching Self-Directed Work Teams. *Mr. Garber received his master's degree in guidance and personnel from St. Bonaventure University.*

ADVENTURES AT WORK OUTLINE

SECTION 1

Name that Movie

Every movie has a title, which is an important factor in its success and marketability. The title sets the tone and describes the movie; it also gives the movie an identity apart from other movies. What title would describe the work you do and the kind of adventure that your audience will experience?

The Current Scene

Movies have scenes that show what is currently occurring in the characters' lives. What is the current scene in your movie? What is going on in your job? Describe it as if it were a movie.

SECTION 2

Supporting Roles

Every movie has certain roles that the characters play. Of course, you play the role of hero or heroine, but the other supporting roles also play an important part in the story's development. In your movie, what supporting roles are important in your job?

Villains

"Villains" do not necessarily have to be people—they can be other aspects of your job or outside sources/influences. In your movie, who are the villains or what are the forces that seem to work against you in your work? How can you neutralize the negative influences these villains exert and have "good" triumph over "bad" in your job?

Suspense

Characters in an adventure movie always experience risk and challenges; this creates the suspense and excitement of the story. At times, the viewers are uncertain as to whether or not the main characters will succeed. Often it is not until the final moments of the movie that the hero finally succeeds in defeating those negative forces. How would you describe the suspense in your job? How might the story of your job change dramatically at a moment's notice? What actions can you as the main character take to help "save the day" and create a happy ending to this movie about your job?

The Chase Scene

The chase scene is also an important element in most adventure movies. In the chase scene, the hero is either chased by or chases the villains. Often, something of great value is being sought, and they defy all obstacles to attain it. Although you may not have actual chase scenes at your job, you pursue things of value in more symbolic ways. If you do not keep up the pursuit, your goal may become out of reach. What would be your chase scene at your work? What are you pursuing? What or who is winning in this chase scene in this movie about your job? How could you change the results of your chase scene?

Section 3

The Conclusion

Typically, a resolution of the conflict or suspense occurs as the movie draws to a close. The end of the movie sets the stage for what might happen to the characters in the future. Usually, as a result of the events in the movie, the characters' lives are changed in significant ways. Often, the characters' relationships with others are strengthened, and they grow closer to one another. What is the conclusion of your movie? What problem or conflict about work was resolved at the end of your movie? How might your relationships with your coworkers be improved as a result of your movie? What new job beginnings might be created as a result of your movie?

Movie Review

Every movie is subjected to the scrutiny of the critics, who tell viewers in no uncertain terms what they think of the movie. Imagine if your job and your job performance were to be evaluated in this way; what would the critics say about it? How many stars would you give your work adventure (with four stars being the highest rating)? What is the reason for the rating?

The Sequel

Often movies will have a sequel for further plot and character development. Will there be an *Adventures at Work II*? What is the reason for having a sequel? How can you make the sequel to your work adventure better than the original?

Congratulations on your work adventure—it is sure to be a winner!

Pfeiffer & Company

522. THAT'S ME:
GETTING TO KNOW YOUR TEAM MEMBERS

Goals

- To kick off a team-building session for an intact work team.
- To encourage team members to learn more about one another.
- To uncover interesting information about one another that can be used and referred to throughout the team-building session.

Group Size

All members of an intact work team.

Time Required

Approximately thirty-five to fifty minutes.

Materials

- A copy of the That's Me Work Sheet for each participant.
- A copy of the That's Me Score Sheet for each participant.
- A pencil and a portable writing surface for each participant.
- A stopwatch for the facilitator's use.

Physical Setting

A room large enough for participants to work independently.

Process

1. The facilitator makes the following introductory remarks:

   "The activity you are about to participate in is called 'That's Me.' It is intended to provide you with an opportunity to find out how well you really know one another."

2. The facilitator distributes the That's Me Work Sheet, pencils, and portable writing surfaces to the participants and explains:

   "You have five minutes to complete the four questions on the That's Me Work Sheet. Please do not let anyone see your responses. This is not a test—just have fun with it. When you are finished, turn your work sheets over and I will collect them from you. Then we will all try to identify the person by his or her answers."

   (Five minutes.)

3. The facilitator collects the work sheets and numbers them sequentially. He or she then distributes copies of the That's Me Score Sheet to each participant with the following instructions:

   "I will read the work sheets for each participant, one at a time. Your job will be to guess who the person is. You will have only fifteen seconds to make your decision and to write down the person's name. You cannot change the name once it is written down. When I call time at the end of fifteen seconds, your pen must be down on the table or you lose one point. If you don't know who the person is, you are better off to guess. Wrong answers will not be penalized. However, only correct answers will receive points. There will be one point awarded for each correct name. The person with the most points wins. Any questions before we start?"

   (Five minutes.)

4. The facilitator reads the first work sheet and then asks each participant group to identify the person and write the appropriate name in the first space. This continues until the facilitator reads all work sheets. (Five to ten minutes.)

5. After the facilitator finishes reading all work sheets, he or she rereads the first one and asks the group to name the person. The facilitator then asks the person who wrote those answers to say "That's me!" The participants who guessed correctly are instructed to circle the answer; those who did not answer correctly are instructed to cross it out. The facilitator continues through the remaining work sheets in the same manner. (Five to ten minutes.)

6. The facilitator leads a concluding discussion based on the following questions:

- How did you feel about completing the work sheet?

- What level of risk did you take with your answers and why? How do you think that compares with the risks that your team members took? What do you wish you had done differently?

- How do you feel about the number of correct answers you had? How do you account for that? What would you like to do differently?

- What answers surprised you about your coworkers? What did you learn about what your coworkers have in common? What strengths about your team have you discovered?

- How can this information help you in working as a team?

(Ten to fifteen minutes.)

Variations

- The questions can be changed to focus on work-related items, such as expectations, concerns, positive aspects of job, favorite customers, motto for team, and so on.

- At the end of Step 4, team members can be asked to predict how many names they have identified correctly.

- The element of competition can be introduced by announcing a "winner" (the person with the most correct answers in Step 5).

- The activity can be extended by pairing up people who did not guess each other correctly and having them complete an additional activity, such as "Building Work Relationships: A Dialogue" in this *Annual*.

Submitted by Debbie Seid.

Debbie Seid received her master's degree in industrial and organizational psychology. Since that time she has worked both as an internal organizational consultant and has founded Excellence Within, a management training and consulting firm. Ms. Seid teaches at the University of Phoenix and San Diego State University and is the author of "Leadership Camp™," a three-day experiential workshop for leaders.

THAT'S ME WORK SHEET

Instructions: Answer each of these questions about yourself. You may respond at whatever level of risk you choose, but avoid answers that might mislead your coworkers.

1. The one thing that nobody in this room realizes about me is...

2. My favorite leisure activity is...

3. A perfect day for me would be to...

4. The actor or actress who should portray me in the movie of my life is...

The 1995 Annual: Volume 1, Training.
Copyright © 1995 by Pfeiffer & Company, San Diego, CA.

THAT'S ME SCORE SHEET

Instructions: The facilitator will read each work sheet and give each one a number. Write the name of the person whom you believe gave those answers next to the corresponding number.

1. _____

2. _____

3. _____

4. _____

5. _____

6. _____

7. _____

8. _____

9. _____

10. _____

11. _____

12. _____

13. _____

14. _____

15. _____

16. _____

Total correct_____

523. The Hand You're Dealt:
Taking a New Perspective on Career Change

Goals

- To provide participants with an opportunity to experience the competitive environment of career change.

- To emphasize the importance of communicating needs and fact finding in the career change process.

- To encourage participants to be willing to go beyond traditional boundaries in seeking resources to assist with their career plan.

Group Size

Up to thirty participants, divided into subgroups of five to eight members each. This activity is designed specifically for people seeking a career change.

Time Required

Approximately forty-five minutes.

Materials

- A deck of poker cards for each subgroup.

- A newsprint poster prepared in advance with the following information:

Rank Order of Poker Hands

- Royal Flush (A, K, Q, J, 10 in the same suit)
- Straight Flush (Five cards in sequence in the same suit)

The 1995 Annual: Volume 1, Training.
Copyright © 1995 by Pfeiffer & Company, San Diego, CA.

- Four of a Kind (Four cards with the same face value)
- Full House (Three cards with the same face value and a pair with another face value)
- Flush (Five cards in the same suit)
- Straight (Five cards in sequence)
- Three of a Kind (Three cards with the same face value)
- Two Pair (A pair of cards with the same face value and another pair with another face value)
- High Card (The card of highest value, with 2 as the lowest and A as the highest)
- A newsprint flip chart and a felt-tipped marker.

Physical Setting

A room large enough so that subgroups can work without disturbing one another. Ideally, a table and chairs should be provided for each subgroup.

Process

1. The facilitator asks the participants to form subgroups of five to eight participants each and explains that they will be playing a game of cards. (Five minutes.)

2. One person in each subgroup is given a deck of cards and is instructed to shuffle the deck several times and have the person to his or her left cut the cards. Meanwhile, the facilitator tells the subgroups that this is a special card game with the following rules:

   - The dealer deals the cards around the subgroup until each member has five cards.

   - Extra cards are to be put aside. *(Note to the facilitator: Do not volunteer the information, but if a participant asks if these cards can be used, say yes.)*

   - Players have three minutes to improve their hands by trading cards with anyone in their subgroup.

   - The winner in each subgroup will be the one with the highest poker hand.

   (Ten minutes.)

3. The facilitator calls time and displays the newsprint poster prepared with the rank order of the poker hands. Each subgroup identifies a winner. The facilitator then leads a concluding discussion and records the career change strategies on a flip chart. The discussion questions might include the following:

- How did the winners win? How do these strategies relate to career change? *(Note to the facilitator: Responses could include knowing what made a winning hand, determining what cards (resources) were needed to win, finding out who had what was needed, communicating needs, and negotiating for cards. Another factor could be the winner was dealt a winning hand and simply was in the right place at the right time. These concepts bridge easily to the process of career development or career change.)*

- Was the extra card pile used? Why or why not? How could this strategy relate to career change? *(Note to the facilitator: Discuss the importance of identifying resources and recognizing artificial boundaries. Often in the career change process, untapped resources are waiting for discovery; those who identify all available resources have the advantage. The old adage "You don't know until you ask" applies here.)*

- A poker game is very competitive. How competitive is the job market? What elements of competition have you experienced? How have you handled that competition?

- What have you learned about the process of career change? How can you apply that to your own (or a future) career search?

(Thirty minutes.)

Variations

- One group can do the exercise while others observe in a group-on-group configuration.

- The game can be complicated by using wild cards.

- The cards from the extra card pile can be made available in a second round if they have not been used. Different results can then be discussed in terms of career change.

- This game could be used in areas other than career change, such as problem solving, accomplishing tasks through negotiation and influence, or effective use of resources.

Submitted by John Powell.

John Powell is a training specialist at Bayfront Medical Center in St. Petersburg, Florida. His work involves developing and instructing in management and leadership programs and facilitating process improvement teams. Mr. Powell specializes in creative learning techniques and has used innovative methods to develop courses in creativity, listening, team building, writing, and presenting. He previously worked as a management trainer for GTE and earned his master's degree in education from Akron University.

524. WORK DIALOGUE:
BUILDING TEAM RELATIONSHIPS

Goals

- To explore the sequence of building from interpersonal to team relationships.

- To provide an opportunity to enhance work relationships through mutual openness and disclosure.

- To allow the participants to practice interpersonal skills related to sharing personal information, taking risks, listening, and giving and receiving feedback.

Group Size

Up to ten pairs of participants. Participants should know one another and have worked together, either as members of an ongoing team or from having worked together in cross-functional teams.

Time Required

Approximately two and one-half hours.

Materials

- A copy of the Work Dialogue Instructions for each participant.

- A copy of Work Dialogue Booklet for each participant. (*Note to the facilitator:* Prepare each Work Dialogue Booklet by cutting along the dashed lines. Assemble the pages in order and staple them along the left side to form a booklet.)

The 1995 Annual: Volume 1, Training.
Copyright © 1995 by Pfeiffer & Company, San Diego, CA.

- Newsprint flip-chart paper and felt-tipped markers for each subgroup.
- Masking tape for posting newsprint.

Physical Setting

- A room, series of rooms, or outdoor area in which the pairs can communicate in relative privacy. Also, a space in which all participants can work in groups of three to five members each, with wall space for posting flip-chart "products."

Process

1. The facilitator introduces the activity by discussing the following points:

   - Today's organizations have shifted (or are shifting) to work relationships based on employee empowerment and participation, teams and groups, interdependence, process orientation, continuous learning, and quality.

   - For example, work relationships occur in self-managed work teams, temporary (or project) teams, total quality management teams, etc.

   - Such relationships require that people be able to deal productively with others in face-to-face situations. Whether working in short- or long-term work groups, individuals need interpersonal skills, understanding of group dynamics, the ability to work creatively with others for extended periods, and the ability to handle ambiguity in both relationships and tasks.

   - To meet the demands of team and group work, people need to have experience and confidence in the skills of relationship building, including being open, taking risks, giving and receiving feedback, listening, and clarifying expectations.

   (Five minutes.)

2. The facilitator has the participants form pairs by any convenient method, asking them to pair up with persons whom they do not know as well as others. (Five minutes.)

3. One copy of the Work Dialogue Instructions and one Work Dialogue Booklet are distributed to each participant. The facilitator reviews the instructions with the participants. (Five minutes.)

4. Each pair is directed to proceed to a private area and to follow the instructions. The participants are told what time to return to the common meeting room. (One and one-half hours.)

5. When the total group has reassembled, the facilitator helps the participants to process the experience by encouraging them to share what they have learned about themselves. [Note: One of the guidelines is confidentiality. It is imperative to ensure that this norm is maintained by permitting each person to talk only about himself or herself, not about his or her partner.] The processing questions may include the following:

   ▪ What was this experience like for you? How did it change as the time progressed?

   ▪ What did you discover about yourself by engaging in this dialogue? What did you discover about the relationship with your partner?

   ▪ What did you learn from this process about building work relationships? What skills are important in building relationships?

   (Ten to fifteen minutes.)

6. After the experience has been processed for individual learnings, the facilitator shifts the focus to implications of the experience for group and team work. The participants are instructed to form groups of three to five members each, depending on the size of the total group (threes if the total group is small and fives if it is large). Dialogue partners should not be in the same group. Each group is given two sheets of flip-chart paper and felt-tipped markers. The discussion groups are asked to extract and list implications for teams resulting from the dialogue experience. The facilitator encourages the participants to focus on the *process* of the dialogue experience. [Once again, participants are reminded not to discuss their dialogue partners' reactions or comments.] (Twenty minutes.)

7. Masking tape is distributed. Each group, in turn, is asked to post its list of implications and briefly to describe the highlights of its discussion. (Ten to twenty minutes.)

8. The facilitator leads a concluding discussion based on the following questions:

   ▪ What are some ways to build team relationships? What things would inhibit building team relationships?

   ▪ What can you apply immediately to a team in which you are a member?

Variations

- If this activity is being used as a team-building activity or with an ongoing work group, the group can then establish norms or expectations for itself for the future based on its members' learnings. The norms can be posted and used periodically as a process check for the group's progress. It is important to emphasize here that relationships are dynamic and that norms and expectations are likely to change over time to accommodate new conditions.

- The participants might want to develop a matrix listing various types of teams and the group-relationship factors that they perceive as particularly salient for those teams. This would help facilitators, leaders, and group members to focus future relationship and team-building activities.

- Pertinent lecturettes (e.g., on group development, the Johari Window, the concept of a "psychological contract," or group norms) can provide team members with a greater understanding of the potential of groups that recognize interpersonal competence in group development and group work.

- Dialogue partners can maintain their relationship throughout a workshop or back on the job as "helping pairs." Periodically, they can get together to explore experiences or concerns relevant to their earlier discussions. It is important to clarify that group-based issues should be brought back to the group for resolution. However, the pair discussions can provide support or insight to members prior to their taking personal observations to the group.

- Self- and/or group-assessment tools can be used as a follow-up to the dialogue. These can help to strengthen each person's self-learning and/or the group's functioning.

- The dialogue can be utilized in team settings. Two options are possible. First, if members have minimal interpersonal or group skills, it is suggested that dialogue partners complete the booklet first. After Step 5, each dialogue pair selects two sentence stems that they think are essential for the team to discuss. Each pair describes why it selected the items. Once the team has had an opportunity to discuss at least one item from each pair, it can return to Step 6 and continue.

  A second option for utilizing the dialogue as a team activity requires that group members have good interpersonal skills, especially in terms of openness and trust. Steps 2, 3, and 4 can be replaced by a team dialogue (a group of sixteen is the maximum size). First, the group discusses the introductory comments for clarity and implications. Then each member starts the discussion of an item by completing the stem. Others follow if they want to. Once discussion slows down for that item, another group member starts discussion of the next item by completing the stem; again other members participate if they choose to. This process continues through all the items or until the allocated time has expired. All members should have an opportunity to initiate an item and to participate in the open discussion. If this is not happening, the facilitator may want to break the group into smaller groups or even pairs, so that each person can participate and learn from the process.

- The activity can be ended after Step 5, after adding a concluding discussion question such as "What have you learned from this experience that you can apply to the team as a whole?"

Submitted by Judith F. Vogt and Karen L. Williams.

Judith Vogt, Ph.D., *works as a consultant in the areas of total quality/continuous learning transition, strategic planning, self-managed work teams, experiential learning, large-group training technologies, leadership, and large systems change. Dr. Vogt has worked with government organizations, universities, service organizations, and national and multi-national corporations. She recently taught at Florida State University and is currently an associate professor of management at Incarnate Word College in San Antonio, Texas. She has published several articles on consulting theory and practice, group and team development, and empowerment. In addition, Dr. Vogt coauthored the book* Empowerment in Organizations.

Karen L. Williams, Ph.D., *is an assistant professor of information systems in the Division of Accounting and Information Systems at the University of Texas at San Antonio. She teaches and conducts research in the fields of information systems/technology management, total quality in information technology projects, and the use of self-directed work teams in information systems. Dr. Williams has ten years of management experience in the pharmaceutical industry and eleven years of experience teaching management at several universities.*

WORK DIALOGUE INSTRUCTIONS

About This Dialogue

The conversation that you are about to begin is intended to help you develop more effective work relationships. Tasks are accomplished more effectively if people who work together have the ability to exchange expertise, ideas, points of view, feelings, and attitudes.

It is also important that you be able to clarify expectations and assumptions that you make about one another in relation to the work to be done. Furthermore, the system's (team, group, division, or organization) culture emerges from interactions that members have with one another.

One purpose of this discussion is to foster greater understanding of others at work. By telling about yourself and by sharing perceptions with another person, you will be working toward a higher level of trust. Trust is the foundation for effective group work, especially in settings that demand coordination, teamwork, creativity, and quality.

Guidelines for This Dialogue

1. The booklet consists of a series of open-ended statements. You and your partner will take turns, each completing the next statement orally. Focus your discussion around work-related issues.

2. All of this discussion is confidential. Do not repeat later what your partner has said during the dialogue.

3. Do not look ahead in the booklet.

4. Do not skip items. Consider each statement in the order in which it is presented.

5. You may decline to respond to any statement.

When you and your partner have finished reading this introduction, turn the page and begin.

Following Up

The items are intended to open a dialogue that can be carried on in your work relationship. You may wish to make definite plans to continue this exchange in the future. Some activities that you may consider follow:

- Go through this dialogue booklet again after about six months.

- Schedule meetings to discuss items and your relationship.

- Contract with each other for support in changing your behavior at work.

WORK DIAGLOGUE BOOKLET
Work Dialogue: Building Team Relationships

Usually, I am the kind of person who...   1

I want to become the kind of person who...   2

When I am feeling anxious in a new work situation, I usually...   3

I am happiest at work when...   4

My greatest area of growth at work is...   5

I am resistant when...   6

I usually react to negative criticism by...   7

I usually react to supportive remarks by...   8

To me, belonging to a team means...   9

When I am in a new work group, I...   10

Briefly discuss how the dialogue is going.   11

When things aren't going well at work, I...   12

Basically, the way I feel about my work is...   13

When I think about your responsibilities, I think that...   14

                                                                     15
The most important skill in developing work relationships is listening. To improve your ability to hear each other, follow these steps: the person whose turn it is completes the following item in two or three sentences; the listener then paraphrases in his or her own words what the speaker has said; then the listener completes the same item, and the other partner paraphrases what he or she has heard.

As a member of a team, I expect...   16

                                                                     17
When each of you has had a turn, share what you may have learned about listening. During this dialogue, you may wish to continue the development of your listening capabilities by paraphrasing what your partner has said.

At work, I'm best at... [18]

In conflict situations between people at work, I usually... [19]

The thing I like best about you is... [20]

I prefer to receive feedback about myself and my work... [21]

The ways I prefer to receive information are... [22]

The kinds of task information I value are... [23]

I prefer to work with people who...   24

My first impression of you was...   25

I think you see me as...   26

What I think you need to know about working with me is... 27

Ten years from now, I...   28

I joined this organization because...   29

The next thing I'm going to try to accomplish at work is... 30

The next step in my career development seems to be... 31

Faced with a conflict between the goals of the organization (division) and your own welfare, I predict that you would... 32

My own personal goals are to... 33

The worst coworker I ever had... 34

When I ask for help at work, I... 35

When someone helps me at work, I...   36

Have a brief discussion of how this dialogue is going so far. How open are   37
you being? How do you feel about your participation up to this point?

The emotion I find most difficult to control at work is...   38

When I offer help at work, I...   39

Your work seems to be...   40

The best colleague I ever had...   41

Listening Check: Paraphrase your partner.   42

- -

The worst boss I ever had...   43

- -

When I am approaching a deadline, I...   44

- -

What team work means to me is...   45

- -

I think my goals and your goals can be achieved if...   46

- -

I think you could help me to...   47

- -

Have a brief discussion of what your responses to the last few items say 48
about what you believe to be valuable in work relationships and teams.

I think our personal goals and our organization's goals can be 49
mutually achieved if...

I think of terms such as "boss," "supervisor," and "manager" as... 50

The best leader I ever worked with... 51

When I see you work with others, I... 52

In a work group, I am most comfortable when my colleagues... 53

In a work group, I feel most comfortable when leadership... 54

My impression of you now is... 55

In a work group, I usually get most involved when... 56

Listening check: Paraphrase your partner. 57

In ambiguous, unstructured situations, I... 58

I like to be a follower when... 59

Pfeiffer & Company

- -

When I have to work with others to accomplish goals, I...   60

- -

My position in this organization...   61

- -

I would like my role in the organization/team to...   62

- -

Together we can...   63

- -

Have a brief discussion of your participation in and reactions to this conversation.   64

- -

525. Levels of Dialogue: Analyzing Communications in Conflict

Goals

- To increase personal effectiveness in resolving conflict through increased awareness and open dialogue.

- To demonstrate one method of becoming aware of the unconscious emotions that can block open and direct communication.

- To enable the participants to receive feedback about their levels of verbal communication, both in sending and receiving messages, and about the congruence of their nonverbal communication.

Group Size

Up to ten trios.

Time Required

One hour and thirty minutes to one hour and forty minutes.

Materials

- One copy of the Levels of Dialogue Theory Sheet for each participant.
- One copy of the Levels of Dialogue Awareness Log for each participant.
- One copy of the Levels of Dialogue Observer Sheet for each participant.
- A pencil for each participant.
- A clipboard or other portable writing surface for each participant.

The 1995 Annual: Volume 1, Training.
Copyright © 1995 by Pfeiffer & Company, San Diego, CA.

- A newsprint poster prepared in advance with the following information:

	Speaker	Listener	Observer
Round 1	A	B	C
Round 2	B	C	A
Round 3	C	A	B

- A newsprint flip chart and a felt-tipped marker.
- Masking tape for posting newsprint.

Physical Setting

A room large enough for pairs to work without disturbing one another. Movable chairs are desirable; tables, desks, or other barriers should be avoided.

Process

1. The facilitator distributes pencils and clipboards, along with copies of the Levels of Dialogue Theory Sheet, the Levels of Dialogue Awareness Log, and the Levels of Dialogue Observer Sheet. He or she presents a lecturette on the Levels of Openness, the Levels of Listening, and the Awareness Log. (Twenty minutes.)

2. Participants are asked to complete the following information on the Levels of Dialogue Awareness Log:

   "Recall several recent conflict situations in which you withheld your feelings, did not tell the whole truth, or were otherwise less than fully open. Write down the reason that you gave yourself for doing this (what you feared would happen). Then identify what you believe is the fear you have about yourself that influenced your decision to withhold in that situation. The distinction between these two different fears is important. For instance, 'I'm afraid I would get fired' is what I feared would happen; 'I'm afraid I couldn't tell my family I lost my job' or 'I'm afraid I couldn't cope with the stress of finding another job' is my fear about myself."

   (Five minutes.)

3. The facilitator assembles the participants in trios and asks each trio to designate one member as "A," another member as "B," and the third member as "C." The facilitator announces that the activity will be con-

ducted in three rounds so that each person will have a turn as speaker, listener, and observer. *(Note to facilitator: If the group does not divide evenly into trios, one or two pairs may be formed; in this case, the role of the observer will be omitted.)* The facilitator posts the prepared newsprint poster of assignments and indicates that in the first round, the "A" participants will be speakers, the "B" participants will be listeners, and the "C" participants will be observers. (Five to ten minutes.)

4. Each speaker is instructed to choose an incident from the Awareness Log that he or she would be willing to discuss within the trio. The speakers are asked to experiment with levels of openness, especially in terms of their fears about what might have happened and their fears about themselves. Similarly, the listeners should focus on Levels 4 and 5 of listening by inviting further explanation and paraphrasing. The observers are asked to identify which levels of openness and listening they notice, at which level the speaker and listener spent the most time, and how nonverbal communication was used. Participants are told that each round of the activity will last for fifteen minutes, including the discussion between the speaker and the listener and the debrief with the observer. The facilitator gives the instruction to begin. (Five minutes.)

5. After ten minutes, the facilitator reminds participants of the time and indicates that they should be concluding their discussions and moving on to the debrief with the observers. Observers are asked to summarize their observations and reactions within their trios, using their notes from the Levels of Dialogue Observer Sheet. *(Note to the facilitator: If the participants are working in pairs, they can share how the experience felt and what they noticed.)* (Fifteen minutes.)

6. The facilitator instructs the members of each trio to switch roles and to repeat the activity two more times, until each members has held the roles of speaker, listener, and observer. The facilitator calls time after each discussion and instructs the participants to debrief as directed in Step 5. (Thirty minutes.)

7. After the final round of the activity, the facilitator reconvenes the total group. The facilitator leads a concluding discussion based on the following questions:

   - How did you react to the experience in the speaker role? The listener role? The observer role?

   - How did the quality of the conversation change over the course of the activity?

   - What did you learn about yourself or your communication patterns?

- What did you learn about levels of dialogue?
- How might you use this learning to improve communications in your daily life?

(Ten to fifteen minutes.)

Variations

- With intact work groups, depending on their sophistication and willingness, each participant may be asked to identify issues or conflicts he or she may have with another team member and then discuss the issue directly with that person using this process. This does increase risk and may require more skill and intervention on the part of the facilitator. Additional time for each discussion is generally needed.

- The role of observer can be eliminated, and the activity can be done in pairs.

Submitted by Gary Copeland.

Gary Copeland, M.P.H., M.H.R.D., is a consultant with University Associates Consulting & Training Services with over 20 years of practical experience managing programs and consulting with organizations in the public and private sectors. He has consulted extensively on communications, leadership, teamwork, increasing individual and group productivity, and strategic planning.

LEVELS OF DIALOGUE THEORY SHEET

Levels of Openness

When "sending" messages, people need to be clear, concise, and direct; they need to describe behaviors or events rather than attribute motives to the actions of others or make character judgments. In *The Truth Option* (Schutz, 1984), Schutz describes "levels of openness" that are dependent on our awareness of our feelings about what is happening (consciousness) and our willingness to express those feelings (courage).

Level -1: Unaware. Sometimes it takes time to become aware of how you feel. Until you become aware of how you feel, you cannot tell others.

Level 0: Withholding. Withholding is the level at which you become aware of how you feel but you are unwilling to express it, at least directly, to the person involved.

Level 1: "You are...." Level 1 openness is the realm of judgments, accusations, and name calling.

Level 2: "About you I feel...." A person who makes a statement of this sort is revealing something about himself or herself rather than making judgments about the character of another person. This invites dialogue and increases understanding.

Level 3: "Because...." At Level 3, you describe the circumstances, events, or behaviors that gave rise to the feelings revealed at Level 2.

Level 4: "Which means...." Everything that happens in our lives has meaning for us. "Meaning," however, is whatever we choose it to be; it therefore is different for each person. This level of openness allows true dialogue to occur and creates an opportunity to clear up the current misunderstanding and to build a stronger relationship for the future.

Level 5: "My fear about myself is...." Level 5 is the deepest level of openness and requires a great deal of self-awareness to achieve. Admittedly, few people reach this level of openness in conversations; however, when they do, the results are often astonishing. As in Level 4, communicating at this level creates a real opportunity for understanding.

Levels of Listening

When receiving messages, people need to listen carefully, make eye contact, and occasionally paraphrase what the other person is saying, as in "What I hear you saying is...." These "levels of listening" (Copeland, 1991) parallel the "levels of openness."

The 1995 Annual: Volume 1, Training.
Copyright © 1995 by Pfeiffer & Company, San Diego, CA.

Level -1: Unaware. The unaware listener is someone more preoccupied with his or her own thoughts or activities than with what you have to say.

Level 0: Avoiding. In contrast, the avoiding listener is acutely aware of the messenger, but does not want to hear what he or she has to say.

Level 1: "No! You are...." When confronted, the Level 1 listener deflects the focus back to the speaker. Immediately deflecting the focus in this manner only serves to escalate emotions and limit the possibility of genuine dialogue, understanding, or resolution.

Level 2: "You shouldn't feel that way." At Level 2 the listener is quick to correct any "inappropriate" feelings being expressed (meaning any feelings that make him or her uncomfortable). This level of "listening" tends to stop communication so that neither party understands the other very well.

Level 3: "Let me tell you...." Level 3 listening is listening for an opportunity to tell your own story; it is characterized by interruptions. The "competitor" tops your story with his or her own successes or calamities, the "debater" corrects your facts, and the "problem solver" waits for an opportunity to solve your problems.

Level 4: "Tell me more." This level is a significant departure from the ones preceding it. At Level 4, the speaker is invited to explain the point, give examples, and discuss how he or she feels and why. Only at this level does a speaker begin to feel that the listener genuinely cares and wants to understand.

Level 5: "What I hear you saying is...." When you paraphrase and reflect back the speaker's concerns, especially when you include the quality and quantity of his or her feelings, that person knows that he or she has been understood. This does not mean that you necessarily agree, but you understand his or her point of view.

Conclusion

Communication is a lively two-way process in which people alternate speaking and listening. Ideally, a person who listens attentively at Level 5 also responds at an appropriate level. The benefits of improving our communications are enormous, and those benefits are attainable. We are most believable when all aspects of our communications are congruent, that is, when our tone, volume, inflection, and body language are in harmony. Not only does this increase effectiveness and productivity, but when we become conscious of the fears that limit us and have the courage to communicate at deeper levels, we can build trusting interpersonal relationships that enrich our lives.

References

Copeland, G. (1991). *Levels of dialogue.* Muir Beach, CA: Will Schutz Associates.

Schutz, W. (1984). *The truth option: A practical technology for human affairs.* Berkeley, CA: Tenspeed Press.

LEVELS OF DIALOGUE AWARENESS LOG

Instructions: Complete this log by recalling several recent conflict situations in which you withheld your feelings, did not tell the whole truth, or were otherwise less than fully open. Write down the reason that you gave yourself for doing this (what you feared would happen). Then identify what you believe is the fear you have about yourself that influenced your decision to withhold in that situation.

Incident (Withhold or Lie)	Fear of What Might Happen (Level 4)	Fear About Myself (Level 5)
1. I pretended I was not upset by what Terry said.	We would get into an argument.	I handle conflict poorly. I say things I don't mean to hurt people's feelings.
2.		
3.		
4.		

Source: *The Awareness Log* by Thompson Barton, 1989, Muir Beach, CA: Will Schutz Associates Update.

LEVELS OF DIALOGUE OBSERVER SHEET

Instructions: Use Table 1 to indicate the level at which the speaker and the listener are operating by placing a checkmark next to that level each time you observe it. Note examples of both verbal and nonverbal behavior whenever possible.

Table 1. Levels of Openness and Listening[1]

Levels of Openness	Speaker Using This Level	Specific Examples	Levels of Listening	Listener Using This Level	Specific Examples
-1. Unaware			-1. Unaware		
0. Withholding			0. Avoiding		
1. "You are..."			1. "No! You are..."		
2. "About you I feel..."			2. "You shouldn't feel that way..."		
3. "Because..."			3. "Let me tell you..."		
4. "Which means..."			4. "Tell me more..."		
5. "My fear about myself is..."			5. "What I hear you saying is..."		

Address the following questions as you debrief the discussion with your partners:

Which levels were used most? How do you account for that?
Which levels were used least? How do you account for that?
What feelings were communicated verbally? Nonverbally?

---

[1] Levels of Openness are based on *The Truth Option* (Schutz, 1984) and Levels of Listening are based on *Levels of Dialogue* (Copeland, 1991). Used with permission.

The 1995 Annual: Volume 1, Training.
Copyright © 1995 by Pfeiffer & Company, San Diego, CA.

526. The Lottery:
Exploring the Impact of Values on Decision Making

Goals

- To allow the participants to experience the dynamics involved in consensus decision making.
- To help the participants to recognize the role of values in decision making

Group Size

Up to five subgroups of five to seven participants each.

Time Required

One hour and fifteen minutes to one hour and thirty-five minutes.

Materials

- One copy of The Lottery Consensus Sheet for each participant.
- A pencil for each participant.
- One copy of The Lottery Observer Sheet for each subgroup.
- A newsprint flip chart and a felt-tipped marker.
- Masking tape for posting newsprint.

Physical Setting

Any room in which subgroups can work without disturbing one another. Movable chairs should be provided.

Process

1. The facilitator introduces the activity along with its goals and assembles the participants into subgroups of five to seven members each. (Five minutes.)

2. The facilitator distributes pencils and copies of The Lottery Consensus Sheet, asks the participants to read the sheet, and answers any questions about the task. Then each subgroup is instructed to choose an observer, who receives a copy of The Lottery Observer Sheet. The subgroups are instructed that they will have thirty minutes to complete the task. (Ten minutes.)

3. After thirty minutes, the facilitator calls time and reconvenes the total group. (Thirty-five minutes.)

4. Each subgroup in turn is instructed to share its rankings, disclose its rationales, and articulate its values and beliefs as clearly as possible. The facilitator records these rankings on newsprint. (Five to fifteen minutes.)

5. The observer for each subgroup shares his or her observations and reactions with the total group. (Five to fifteen minutes.)

6. The facilitator leads a concluding discussion based on the following questions:

   - How did you feel about working on this task?

   - What types of behaviors helped the subgroup in its consensus seeking? What behaviors hindered?

   - How did individual values affect the consensus-seeking activity?

   - What effects of group values do you see in the rankings?

   - What have you learned about how values affect decision making? How does that fit with your experience?

   - How can you improve your individual or team decision making with these learnings?

   (Fifteen minutes.)

Variations

- The choices for how to spend the money could be changed to create more controversial discussions. For example, someone might want to give all of the money to an abortion clinic or to support a revolutionary government in another country.

- The subgroups could simply be told to make a decision without the instruction that it be by consensus.

- Individuals could rank the choices first before proceeding to the group task.

Submitted by R. Glenn Ray.

R. Glenn Ray, Ph.D., *is a professor of leadership and the director of the Institute for Education and Training for Business at Marietta College. He consults with a variety of organizations in the areas of team development, interpersonal communication processes, problem-solving and decision-making techniques, implementation of self-directed work teams, facilitation skills, and leadership skills. Dr. Ray has presented and published a number of articles on team development and organizational communication processes.*

THE LOTTERY CONSENSUS SHEET

The Situation

Five friends who work together in an office have been playing the lottery together for three years. Every week, each person pays in five dollars to purchase tickets. Three months ago, one of the five lottery players, Chris, decided to quit the group. The other group members begged Chris to continue playing and agreed to Chris's condition: The distribution of any winnings would be based on the consensus of the group. If the group could not come to consensus, then the money would be given to the federal government to reduce the national debt.

Last week the group won ten million dollars! The following positions have been identified by individual group members:

Chris: Wants to hold a winner-take-all drawing.

Dale: Wants to give all of the money to environmental causes.

Pat: Wants to use all of the money to create a foundation to bring art and music to elementary schools.

Robin: Wants to purchase a villa in the south of France and allocate shares of vacation time equally to all group members.

Kelly: Wants all of the members to invest in a computer-chip manufacturing company.

The Task

Use consensus decision making to rank the suggestions from best to worst (1 to 5, respectively). It is important to remember that you must reach a consensus regarding the ranking given to each item. "Consensus" means that each member of the subgroup agrees to implement the plan. Coercion and methods of conflict avoidance such as averaging, voting, and trading agreements between individuals are not allowed.

Name	Rank
Chris	
Dale	
Pat	
Robin	
Kelly	

The 1995 Annual: Volume 1, Training.
Copyright © 1995 by Pfeiffer & Company, San Diego, CA.

Be prepared for a spokesperson to explain the rationale behind the ranking and the values inherent in the rationale.

Rationale:

Values:

THE LOTTERY OBSERVER SHEET

Instructions: Observe your subgroup's decision-making process and make notes in the following areas:

How did your subgroup approach the task?

What aspect of the task caused the most discussion?

Which decisions were made first? Last?

How did the subgroup follow the guidelines for consensus decision making?

The 1995 Annual: Volume 1, Training.
Copyright © 1995 by Pfeiffer & Company, San Diego, CA.

527. Values, Visions, and Missions: Using Personal Strategic Planning

Goals

- To introduce the participants to the strategic planning process as it can be applied in their own lives and careers.
- To offer the participants an opportunity to explore and define their individual directions in terms of life and career issues.
- To help each participant define his or her personal values and create a personal vision statement and a mission statement.
- To offer the participants a chance to give and receive feedback about their values, their vision statements, and their proposed mission statements.

Group Size

Any number of subgroups of three participants each. If necessary, one or two subgroups may have two or four members each.

Time Required

Approximately one and one-half to two hours.

Materials

- A copy of the Values, Visions, and Missions Work Sheet for each participant.
- A pencil for each participant.

The 1995 Annual: Volume 1, Training.
Copyright © 1995 by Pfeiffer & Company, San Diego, CA.

Physical Setting

A room large enough so that the subgroups can work without disturbing one another. Each subgroup should have chairs and a table (or movable desks). If tables or desks are not available, the facilitator may distribute clipboards or other portable writing surfaces.

Process

1. The facilitator introduces personal strategic planning as an adaptation of strategic planning for organizations. Each participant is given a pencil and a copy of the Values, Visions, and Missions Work Sheet and is asked to read Parts 1 and 2. After all participants have finished reading, the facilitator leads a discussion about Parts 1 and 2, ensuring that the participants understand the basic process of personal strategic planning as well as the terms "values," "vision statement," and "mission statement." (Twenty minutes.)

2. Subgroups of three members each are formed. Each participant is instructed to work individually to complete Parts 3, 4, and 5 of the work sheet. (Approximately twenty minutes.)

3. After all participants have completed Parts 3, 4, and 5, the facilitator invites the members of each subgroup to share their values, vision statements, and mission statements and to ask for feedback on the consistency among these components and whether their mission statements meet the criteria listed in Part 5. *The facilitator emphasizes that all sharing is to be done on a voluntary basis; participants may share as much or as little as they wish.* (Thirty minutes).

4. The participants are instructed to complete Part 6 of their work sheets. (Five to ten minutes.)

5. The facilitator summarizes the initial stages of the planning process (Parts 3 through 6 of the work sheet), outlines the subsequent steps of the process (setting specific goals and developing strategies to achieve those goals, as described in Part 7), briefly reviews the tips in Part 8, and encourages the participants to establish goals and strategies on their own after they leave the training session. (Five to ten minutes.)

6. The facilitator leads a concluding discussion by asking questions such as the following:

   - What was it like for you to write your values, vision statement, and mission statement? What was it like to share them with others?

- How did your subgroup discussions help in the process of creating a final mission statement?

- What have you learned about yourself? What have you learned about personal strategic planning? What have you learned about the importance of sharing your vision and mission statements with others?

- What will you do differently in your personal or professional life now that you have completed this activity?

- How will you follow up on your vision and mission statements to continue the process of personal strategic planning? What are your plans for sharing your vision and mission statements with significant others?

(Fifteen minutes).

7. The participants are encouraged to review their values, vision statements, and mission statements from time to time and to make adjustments as necessary. The facilitator again emphasizes the importance of developing goals and strategies after the training session and reminds the participants of the first item in Part 2 of the work sheet: "Strategic thinking is an ongoing process, not something you do once and then abandon." (Five minutes.)

Variations

- At the conclusion of the activity, the facilitator may invite the participants to post their final mission statements and to review the posted work.

- The work sheet may be completed by an individual working alone or by two partners who provide feedback and help each other.

- Posters with vision and mission statements may be prepared and displayed as examples.

- The process may be extended using Part 7 of the work sheet. As feedback can be an important part of goal setting, the facilitator may invite the participants to share some of their goals in their subgroups.

- If this activity is used with an ongoing work group, personal mission statements may be discussed in light of the team's mission or the organization's mission.

Submitted by Chuck Kormanski.

Chuck Kormanski, Ed.D., is a counselor for the Career Development and Placement Service at the Altoona Campus of The Pennsylvania State University. He counsels and teaches college students, is involved in organizational training and development, and does research in leadership and team building. Dr. Kormanski is a past president of the Association for Specialists in Group Work. He is a member in the American Counseling Association, the Society of Industrial and Organizational Psychology, and the American Society for Training and Development.

VALUES, VISIONS, AND MISSIONS WORK SHEET[1]

PART 1: Definition of Personal Strategic Planning

Personal strategic planning is the process by which you create a vision of your future and then determine specific steps to take to achieve that future. The process begins with clarifying *values,* writing a *vision statement,* and then developing a *mission statement.* Definitions of these terms are as follows:

- *Values:* "Concepts, principles, or standards that drive one's decisions and actions." Examples of values are honesty, persistence, dependability, self-sufficiency, and faith.

- *A vision statement:* "A statement of three or four sentences describing a desired future—not a predicted future." Here is an example of a vision statement (stated as if the vision has already been achieved, so that it is positive and powerful): "I am a person who is peaceful and an example to others of that peace, which comes from faith in God. I am considered to be an inspirational teacher of great integrity. I lead a simple life style that includes plenty of time for myself, my family, and my friends as well as service to others."

- *A mission statement:* "A succinct, easy-to-remember statement that provides direction for one's life." Here is an example of a very short mission statement developed from the sample vision statement quoted above: "I am committed to living in accordance with my faith in God, maintaining a happy marriage, and being a loving and supportive parent. In my professional life, I seek to empower high school students by providing quality teaching while adhering to my religious principles. I want to live a simple life style." Note that a mission statement may be lengthier if desired, but brevity is important.

During this process it is critical to ensure consistency between values, the vision statement, and the mission statement. If these three components are not consistent, it is not possible to devise a workable plan.

Notes:

---

[1] The process of personal strategic planning described in this work sheet is based on *Shaping Your Organization's Future: Frogs, Dragons, Bees, and Turkey Tails* by T.M. Nolan, L.D. Goodstein, and J.W. Pfeiffer, 1993, San Diego, CA: Pfeiffer & Company.

PART 2: Personal Strategic Planning Principles

Here are some principles to keep in mind while doing personal strategic planning:

1. Strategic thinking is an ongoing process, not something you do once and then abandon. Therefore, the process allows you to adapt to change.

2. Change is a given, not a choice. The choice you have is whether or not you want to influence the change.

3. You cannot predict the future, but you can influence it by creating a vision statement.

4. The future is not what it used to be. At one time, the immediate future looked very much like the present. Today change is so rapid that even the immediate future can be very different from the present.

5. There are no permanent solutions, only temporary ones.

6. Any opportunity you fail to take may never come your way again.

7. Decision making includes action.

8. You cannot do everything at once.

9. The most difficult decision you make today will not affect you until tomorrow. A strategic decision will not have a major impact on today's activities, but it will place you in a position of leverage whereby you can influence tomorrow's activities.

10. Without a vision of the future, a person becomes directionless.

Notes:

PART 3: Collecting Information for Your Vision and Mission Statements

To collect information to be used in creating your vision and mission statements, write answers to the following four questions:

1. List some core values that have been important to you throughout your life.

2. Describe the person you want to be and the life style you want to lead.

3. Describe the career you want and the professional person you aspire to become.

4. Describe your distinctive competency.[2]

---

[2] Your "distinctive competency" is the quality or attribute that distinguishes you from other people and makes you unique. You might want to think of it as your most significant characteristic, skill, or ability.

PART 4: Creating Your Vision Statement

How would you like to see yourself three to five years from now? Your next task is to write a statement of what you envision for yourself.

Ford and Lippitt (1988) describe how to approach the process of creating a vision statement:

> While working on your vision, try to suspend your internal critic as well as any inclination to be modest or prudent. At this point don't concern yourself with whether your vision is achievable. This is a time to entertain notions of greatness, to reach as far as your desires will take you. (p. 8)

Use the space below to describe your desired future in general terms. Write about three or four sentences.

PART 5: Writing Your Mission Statement, First Draft

■ Before you begin work on a mission statement, review the following ten criteria and make notes about items to include in your own statement.

Ten Criteria for Evaluating Mission Statements[3]

Your mission statement should:

1. Be clear and understandable to significant others.

2. Be brief enough to keep it in mind.

3. Specify your career direction.

4. Include a short description of your preferred life style.

5. Reflect your distinctive competency.

6. Be broad enough to allow flexibility in implementation—but not so broad that it lacks focus.

7. Serve as a guide for making personal and career decisions.

8. Reflect your values, beliefs, and philosophy.

9. Be achievable (challenging and realistic).[4]

10. Serve as a source of energy for you.

---

[3] From *Applied Strategic Planning: A Comprehensive Guide* (p. 188) by L.D. Goodstein, T.M. Nolan, and J.W. Pfeiffer, 1992, San Diego, CA: Pfeiffer & Company. Adapted by permission.

[4] Think of your mission statement as your vision made realistic.

■ Write a rough draft of your mission statement, keeping in mind the ten criteria on the previous page.

PART 6: Writing Your Mission Statement, Final Draft

Now write a final draft of your mission statement.

PART 7: Devising Goals and Strategies to Achieve Your Vision

After you have written the final draft of your mission statement, you are ready to develop goals and strategies.

A goal is an objective that leads to achieving some portion of your vision. It must be consistent not only with your values and your mission statement but also with any other goals that you set.

A goal is much more specific than your vision or even your mission statement. For example, if your vision includes "Having a successful career in graphic design," then one of your goals may be "In the next two years, complete (with a final grade of at least B) the one-unit course entitled 'Photoshop for Publications' through the University of California at San Diego Extension."

Note the details included in the goal: a time limit (in the next two years), a criterion for success (with a final grade of at least B), the amount of credit earned on completion of the course (one unit), the specific title of the course ("Photoshop for Publications"), and the institution offering the course (the University of California at San Diego Extension).

It is easy to see how realizing even one portion of your vision may require setting many such goals.

Strategies

A strategy is a method or technique for achieving a goal. Just as realizing your vision will require setting a number of goals, achieving a single goal may require using a number of strategies. For example, achieving the goal of attending the course in photoshop may necessitate such strategies as changing job hours to accommodate course work, making arrangements to carpool to and from the course with a coworker, arranging for a babysitter to watch the children so that evening classes can be attended, and so on.

The structure on the following page will help you to become acquainted with the procedure of setting goals and devising strategies to achieve those goals. For the purpose of this activity, select three goals in connection with realizing some component of your vision and outline the strategies necessary for achieving those goals. (*Note:* To achieve all components of your vision, you will need to repeat this procedure for each component.)

Goal

Strategies

PART 8: Getting the Most from Personal Strategic Planning

The following are tips for getting the most from personal strategic planning:

- Keep reviewing your vision and mission statements from time to time. Make alterations as necessary.

- If your picture of a desired future changes, remember to change your vision and mission statements and then your goals and strategies as necessary. Be willing to adjust your vision and mission statements (and associated goals and strategies) if you need/want to.

- Keep your vision and mission statements posted in your office, in a computer file, on your refrigerator, or in any other prominent place where you will see them frequently.

- When you are making an important life or career decision, refer to your vision and mission statements and make sure that the decision you are contemplating is consistent with your intended direction.

- Share your vision and mission statements with significant others and ask for feedback about ways to achieve your vision. If you uncover inconsistencies between your vision and what significant others want/expect from you, work on those inconsistencies so that they do not interfere with meeting your goals.

- Keep on the lookout for opportunities that will help you reach your goals. This may include picking up related books and reading them, attending seminars and workshops, joining groups or organizations, and so on.

- Check on your progress toward goals at least every three months.

Notes:

References

Ford, G.A., & Lippitt, G.L. (1988). *Creating your future: A guide to personal goal setting.* San Diego, CA: Pfeiffer & Company.

Goodstein, L.D., Nolan, T.M., & Pfeiffer, J.W. (1992). *Applied strategic planning: A comprehensive guide.* San Diego, CA: Pfeiffer & Company.

Nolan, T.M., Goodstein, L.D., & Pfeiffer, J.W. (1993). *Shaping your organization's future: Frogs, dragons, bees, and turkey tails.* San Diego, CA: Pfeiffer & Company.

528. LET'S COME TO ORDER: GETTING DOWN TO BUSINESS

Goals

- To acquaint the participants with the basics of an effective task-oriented meeting.

- To give the participants an opportunity to participate in or observe a task-oriented meeting and then to give or receive feedback on the effectiveness of that meeting.

- To demonstrate the effects of process (how members interact with one another) on task and vice versa.

- To develop the participants' awareness of behaviors that facilitate or hinder task completion during a meeting.

Group Size

Fifteen to twenty participants (ten meeting participants and five to ten observers).

Time Required

Approximately one and one-half hours.

Materials

- Ten copies of the Let's Come to Order Meeting Simulation for the meeting participants.

- A set of ten envelopes (4⅛" x 9½" or similar size), each containing one of the ten Let's Come to Order Role Descriptions.

- One set of observer materials for each observer, consisting of the following materials:
  - One copy of the Let's Come to Order Meeting Simulation.
  - One copy of the Let's Come to Order Observer Sheet.
  - One copy of each of the ten Let's Come to Order Role Descriptions.
  - A pencil.
  - A clipboard or other portable writing surface.
- A newsprint flip chart and a felt-tipped marker for the meeting participants (for the scribe's use).
- Masking tape for posting newsprint.

Physical Setting

This activity relies on a group-on-group configuration, which consists of two groups of participants: One group forms a circle and actively participates in an activity; the other group forms a circle around the first group and observes the first group's activity. Therefore, the room that is used should be large enough to accommodate the two circles of participants and should include movable chairs.

Process

1. The facilitator explains the goals of the activity.

2. The participants are assembled into two circles. The inner circle consists of ten participants who will take part in the meeting simulation, and the outer circle consists of five to ten participants who will observe the meeting simulation. (Five minutes.)

3. Each observer is given one set of observer materials (see Materials). The observers are asked to read all of the information they have been given.

4. The facilitator gives the meeting participants a newsprint flip chart, a felt-tipped marker, and masking tape (for the scribe's use). The meeting participants are given copies of the Let's Come to Order Meeting Simulation and are asked to read it. Then each meeting participant selects one of the ten envelopes, each of which contains one of the Let's Come to Order Role Descriptions. Each meeting participant reads his or her own role silently. The facilitator then elicits and answers questions *about the meeting task only*. (Ten minutes.)

5. The meeting participants are told that they have thirty minutes in which to conduct their meeting and are instructed to begin. (Thirty minutes.)

6. At the end of the thirty-minute period, the facilitator asks the meeting participants to stop their meeting and to abandon their roles. The meeting participants are asked to discuss briefly *(not playing their meeting roles)* what went well and what they would change about how the meeting was conducted. (Ten minutes.)

7. The meeting participants and meeting observers are asked to switch places so that the observers are in the inner circle and the participants are in the outer circle. The observers are asked to share and discuss their observations, using their observer sheets as a starting point. (Fifteen to twenty minutes, depending on the number of observers.)

8. The facilitator leads a concluding discussion by asking the following questions:

   - Other than those already mentioned, what meeting roles, tools, or procedures were helpful?

   - Other than those already mentioned, what interpersonal behaviors helped task completion? Which ones hindered?

   - How would you describe the relationship between process and task during a task-oriented meeting?

   - How will you apply what you have learned in future meetings?

   (Ten to fifteen minutes.)

Variations

- The meeting role assignments (meeting manager, scribe, and timekeeper) could be eliminated, retaining only those individuals' personal characteristics. This variation would give participants more opportunity to discover what is missing in terms of roles, tools, and so on.

- A budget and blueprint could be added for the meeting participants to work with in conducting their meeting.

- The number of meeting participants could be reduced by eliminating those roles not crucial to the activity.

- The activity could begin without the meeting manager, scribe, and timekeeper. Halfway through the meeting, the facilitator could introduce and assign those roles.

Submitted by Michele M. Moomaugh.

Michele M. Moomaugh is a consultant and trainer based in San Diego, California. She consults with local, national, and international organizations, both public and private. She specializes in the management of systems and organizational change, executive coaching, leadership/management development, and employee training. In addition to operating her consulting business, Ms. Moomaugh is the coordinator for the organizational-effectiveness component of an urban community-services program at San Diego State University. Having lived and traveled extensively in other countries, Ms. Moomaugh applies her understanding of cultural differences and diversity issues in her work with organizations.

LET'S COME TO ORDER MEETING SIMULATION

During this activity you will have an opportunity to participate in a simulation to discover important information about how you participate in a meeting. You and the nine other meeting participants are to role play members of a task force created by the director of your department, "Department Z."

Department Z, which is located downtown, is a department of the local city government. In about three months the department will be moving to another downtown location approximately six blocks from its current location. The department is moving because it has outgrown its current space and needs to move into a larger facility in order to continue to respond to the requests of citizens and other departments in a timely and effective manner.

This is the first meeting of the task force in response to the task generally outlined by the department director in the memo on the next page. You will each be given other instructions in separate envelopes. Other than that, you are on your own to decide what to do at your first meeting to start work on the task that you have been charged with.

You will be told how much time you have for your meeting. After you have held your meeting and critiqued it, the people who have observed the meeting will also critique it while you listen.

Once you have read this page, you are to assume the character of a task-force member and a participant in the upcoming meeting. Do not abandon this identity until you are instructed to do so.

Memo from Department Director

To: Relocation Task Force, Department Z
From: A.J. Reed, Director
Regarding: Recommendations for move to new building

As you know, we will be moving to another facility downtown in three months. This is a wonderful opportunity for us to rethink how we want to set up our department: Are there better ways for us to organize the layout of our work areas, desks, office equipment, and so on?

Because this is a complex and challenging task, I've decided to generate more involvement in the decision making by asking each of you to serve on the task force as a representative for the entire department.

Plan to meet as often as necessary for the next six weeks to study and recommend to me *the best possible layout for our new location.* Blueprints will be made available to you, along with the budget and other information about the new facility. Your recommendations will be seriously considered by me and the Buildings Division manager assigned to coordinate our move.

When you meet, consider the following topics:

- Should the clerical staff be centrally located or dispersed throughout the area we have been given? Which works best—centralized or decentralized clerical staffing?

- Should we consider small offices (with doors) shared by two or three people or individual cubes with acoustical walls and no doors?

- Should we have a large conference room to be used by everyone, or should we have a smaller conference room so that space can be dedicated to an employee lounge?

- Should we go with our traditional beige walls or consider a nontraditional color?

I am really open to creative thinking on these challenging and sensitive concerns, so I hope you can come up with some fair way to decide such issues for our department. Once our new layout is in place, it will be a long time before we'll have such an opportunity again, so please be thoughtful about your recommendations and stay within the financial limits you'll be given.

In order to help you get started, I've assigned a meeting manager, a scribe, and a timekeeper. Those responsibilities are described as follows:

The 1995 Annual: Volume 1, Training.
Copyright © 1995 by Pfeiffer & Company, San Diego, CA.

Meeting Manager—Runs the meeting, keeps everyone involved, makes sure that the group stays on one topic at a time, ensures that the predetermined method of reaching decisions is adhered to, maintains the time schedule, and leads the post-meeting evaluation.

Scribe—Uses a newsprint flip chart and a felt-tipped marker to record participants' thoughts and to keep track of ideas.

Timekeeper—Monitors the participants' use of time and periodically notifies the meeting manager of the time (according to previously agreed-on time increments).

LET'S COME TO ORDER ROLE DESCRIPTIONS

ROLE 1

Meeting Manager

You are not quite sure how to go about accomplishing the assignment given to you and your task-force members, but you feel strongly that everyone should have a voice in the recommendations made. You hope that no one's ideas get too crazy. You also are aware that to enhance involvement in future meetings, it would be a good idea to take five minutes at the end of this meeting to assess its effectiveness. You will make sure that this time is taken.

At the beginning of the meeting, you should announce that you are the meeting manager, but *do not share the information in the previous paragraph.*

ROLE 2

Scribe

This is your chance to show people not only how well you can capture their ideas, but also how influential you can be. Be sure to participate actively in the discussion and make your opinions known.

At the beginning of the meeting, you should announce that you are the scribe, but *do not share the information in the previous paragraph.*

ROLE 3

Timekeeper

You are very punctual by nature and are not inclined to let people be sloppy about how they use their time. Furthermore, you have some definite opinions about the color that the walls should be: The task force should definitely stay with the beige used in the current offices.

At the beginning of the meeting, you should announce that you are the timekeeper, but *do not share the information in the previous paragraph.*

ROLE 4

Creative Thinker

You see the task-force project as a wonderful chance to turn the usual conservative approach of the department upside down. During the meeting you plan to push for some creative ways of addressing the issues mentioned in the director's memo. You know that a way to unleash creativity is to take care of process concerns up-front (how the meeting will be conducted, how people will be recognized and make comments, how decisions will be made, and so on).

Do not share this information with anyone.

ROLE 5

Clerical Representative

You are concerned that other department members seldom take the needs of the clerical employees into consideration, so you plan to work hard during the meeting to represent the clerical staff well. You will push for the decentralization of the clerical staff, because you believe that your fellow clerical employees would not like to be put into a centralized "pen," as you call it.

Do not share this information with anyone.

ROLE 6

Middle Manager

You do not care what anyone else wants in the new location as long as you can have your own office with a window.

Do not share this information with anyone.

ROLE 7

Quiet Employee

You cannot believe that you have been assigned to this important task force, and your tendency is to be quiet during the meeting and see what the others say and do.

Do not share this information with anyone.

ROLE 8

Vocal Employee

The upcoming meeting is your chance to be heard, so you plan to take every opportunity to talk. After all, your ideas are usually pretty good, and you take seriously the director's effort to involve others in the relocation. You do know that you need to have everyone agree on the desired objectives of the meeting.

Do not share this information with anyone.

ROLE 9

Disinterested Employee

You have lots of important things that you should be doing instead of attending the upcoming meeting. In fact, you believe that most meetings are a waste of time. Consequently, you plan to work discreetly on other things while the task force meets.

Do not share this information with anyone.

ROLE 10

Skeptical Employee

You are not happy about being on this task force, and you hope that this meeting is the only one you will have to attend. In addition, you are skeptical that the task force is really empowered to do anything other than go through the motions just to make the department director look good.

Do not share this information with anyone.

LET'S COME TO ORDER OBSERVER SHEET

Instructions: Attached are copies of all handouts being used by the ten people participating in the meeting simulation. *Review the remainder of this sheet and all handouts before the simulation begins.*

During the simulation you will be observing the meeting interactions and completing this sheet, which deals with your observations. Whenever possible, jot down an example from the meeting to support your opinion. *Note:* You do not have to answer all of the questions below; simply use them as guidelines for your critique.

After the meeting simulation ends, you will be asked to meet with the other observers to discuss your critiques while the meeting participants listen.

PROCESS

1. What seemed helpful about the roles assigned by the director (meeting manager, scribe, and timekeeper)?

2. What meeting tools, techniques, or procedures were effective in the meeting?

3. How would you describe the participation level of the group?

TASK

How would you describe the quantity and quality of work accomplished during the meeting, even though there were time constraints?

RECOMMENDATIONS

What would you have the meeting participants do differently if they were to meet again?

529. THE HELPING HAND: SUPPORTING TEAMMATES' GOALS

Goals

- To offer members of an intact team an opportunity to gain the support of their teammates in achieving goals.
- To offer members of an intact team an opportunity to offer feedback about one another's strengths.
- To offer participants a chance to state their own perceived strengths.

Group Size

All members of an intact work team.

Time Required

Forty-five minutes to one hour, depending on the size of the team.

Materials

- One copy of The Helping Hand Outline for each participant.
- Several sheets of blank paper and a pencil for each participant.

Physical Setting

Any room in which the participants can be seated comfortably. If tables are not available, portable writing surfaces should be provided.

Process

1. The facilitator announces that the participants are about to take part in an activity through which they can identify goals that they see for themselves as well as the strengths they bring.

2. The facilitator gives each participant a copy of The Helping Hand Outline, several sheets of blank paper, and a pencil. The facilitator asks each participant to use the "Goals/Challenges" section of the handout to write down one or more personal challenges or goals that he or she wants to address in the next few months. These challenges or goals should be ones that he or she is willing to share with the other participants. (Five minutes.)

3. The facilitator gives the following instructions:

   "Each of you in turn will share aloud his or her goals or challenges. As you share, your teammates will make notes for themselves about the qualities and strengths that you have that will help you to achieve these objectives. Be sure to use the blank paper for your notes about your teammates."

4. Each participant in turn shares his or her personal goals or challenges as the other participants listen and take notes. The facilitator allows time between participants for the other participants to complete their notes. (Ten to fifteen minutes.)

5. After all participants have shared, they are given the following instructions:

   "On the upper portion of your copy of The Helping Hand Outline, trace your own hand. Leave your own copy of the outline at your place. Take the notes that you have written about your teammates and go around to each person's hand outline. Within that person's hand outline itself, write down the strengths you have observed about that person."

   (Ten to fifteen minutes.)

6. When all participants have finished, the facilitator invites them to take their places and read the comments that their teammates have noted. Each participant is asked to share one or more of the comments with the group as a whole. (Ten minutes.)

7. The facilitator leads a discussion of how the strengths that have been identified can help to meet the opportunities and challenges that lie ahead. He or she might prompt discussion with questions such as the following:

- How did you feel when you shared a personal challenge or goal with your teammates?

- How did it feel to read the comments that your teammates noted about you?

- What have you learned about team support in achieving personal goals?

- How can you use the support of your teammates as "helping hands" along your path?

(Ten to fifteen minutes.)

Variations

- Members of an intact work team can use this process to identify challenges for the team and the strengths that each member adds to the team.

- In a full-fledged feedback session, a second hand could be drawn and areas of growth listed.

- Members can focus on individual goals or challenges that they face in the team.

Submitted by Kathleen Kreis.

Kathleen Kreis, Ed.D., is the Director of English for the Buffalo Public Schools. She also conducts workshops on the topics of job satisfaction and burnout, communication skills, Enneagram Personality Theory, and employee motivation. She has written many articles that have appeared in such journals as The Clearing House, Teaching K-8, and The Executive Educator. Dr. Kreis earned her degree from the State University of New York at Buffalo.

THE HELPING HAND OUTLINE

Goals/Challenges:

530. THEY SAID, WE SAID:
EXPLORING INTERGROUP-CONFLICT RESOLUTION

Goals

- To offer the participants a process and behaviors for resolving intergroup conflicts.
- To provide the participants with an opportunity to practice or observe intergroup-conflict resolution in a safe environment.

Group Size

All members of two ongoing work teams.

Time Required

One hour and forty minutes.

Materials

- Blank paper, a pencil, and a clipboard or other portable writing surface for each of four volunteers (see Step 7).
- A newsprint flip chart and a felt-tipped marker.
- Masking tape for posting newsprint.

Physical Setting

A room that will accommodate a group-on-group configuration. A group-on-group configuration consists of two groups of participants: One group forms a circle and actively participates in an activity; the other group forms a circle around the first group and observes the first group's activity. In this activity, four participants engage in a role play in the inner circle while the remaining participants observe in the outer circle. Movable chairs should be provided for the participants, and plenty of wall space should be available for posting newsprint.

Process

1. The facilitator introduces the goals of the activity.

2. The participants are asked to contribute examples of intergroup-conflict issues or situations that they have experienced or are experiencing. The facilitator clarifies that the examples *need not* involve these two particular teams, but *may* involve these two teams if the participants wish; however, the examples must be situations that the participants would not object to role playing. As the participants contribute sample conflict situations, the facilitator records the highlights of each situation in neutral terms on newsprint. He or she then posts each completed newsprint sheet. (Ten minutes.)

3. The facilitator chooses one of the conflict situations and asks for two volunteers from each work team. The volunteers are instructed to be seated in a circle in the middle of the room with the remaining participants seated around them.

4. The volunteers from one work team role play one side of the situation, and the volunteers from the other work team role play the other side of the same situation. The volunteers are asked to spend ten minutes role playing the chosen situation and coming to some resolution of it. The remaining participants serve as observers and are asked to note their impressions of behaviors that helped and those that hindered resolving the conflict. (Ten minutes.)

5. After ten minutes the facilitator stops the role play and asks the four volunteers to discuss answers to the following questions:

   ▪ How do you feel about the resolution of the role play?

   ▪ What did you agree to?

   ▪ Which behaviors helped to resolve the conflict? Which behaviors hindered resolution?

   As the volunteers discuss their answers, the facilitator writes their comments on newsprint. After the volunteers have completed their discussion, the observing participants are asked to contribute their impressions about what was agreed to, which behaviors helped, which behaviors did not help, and the resolution of the role play; these comments also are recorded. All newsprint is posted so that the participants can review the content later. (Twenty minutes.)

6. The facilitator makes the following comments about the process involved in resolving intergroup conflict:

"When two groups disagree and are unable to resolve their differences, it is often because each individual group's needs were not listened to or met. A successful approach to intergroup conflict resolution provides two things: (1) an opportunity for each group to state and clarify what it needs and (2) a commitment from each group to listen to and try to understand the other group's needs.

"After both groups have stated and clarified their needs and listened to and understood the other group's needs, the two groups explore through back-and-forth dialogue how to meet both sets of needs. They look for opportunities to meet both groups' needs simultaneously. Also, they explore the reason behind each group's needs: Why does the other group want a particular thing? What will that thing provide? Sometimes discovering the reasons behind needs can be the key to a successful resolution.

"Once a resolution has been determined, both groups should summarize aloud what they have agreed to do. Sharing summaries ensures that both groups are taking away the same action plan and are committed to carrying out that plan."

As the facilitator talks, he or she outlines this process on newsprint, posts the newsprint prominently, and then elicits and answers questions about the process. (Ten minutes.)

7. The facilitator chooses another situation to role play using the process just described; he or she asks for two different volunteers from each work team. The new volunteers are instructed to be seated in the inner circle. In addition, all four volunteers are given blank paper, a pencil, and a clipboard or other portable writing surface. Volunteers are told that they will spend a couple of minutes making notes on his or her own team's needs *before* beginning the role play and instructed to make notes on the other team's needs *during* the role play. The facilitator reminds the volunteers to make sure their teams' needs are stated and understood, to make sure they hear and understand the other team's needs, and to explore ways of meeting both sets of needs.

8. After allowing a few minutes for the volunteers to make notes, the facilitator asks them to spend ten minutes role playing the new situation. (Approximately fifteen minutes.)

9. After the role play has been in progress for ten minutes, the facilitator stops it and invites the four volunteers to discuss answers to the same questions asked in connection with the previous role play:

- How do you feel about the resolution of the role play?

- What did you agree to?

- Which behaviors helped to resolve the conflict? Which behaviors hindered resolution?

Again the facilitator writes the volunteers' comments on newsprint. Subsequently, the observers share their impressions about what was agreed to, which behaviors were helpful, which behaviors were not helpful, and the resolution of the role play; these comments also are recorded. All newsprint is posted next to the sheets with the comments on the previous role play. (Twenty minutes.)

10. The facilitator leads a discussion comparing the two role plays and concluding the activity. The following questions may be helpful:

- How did the second role play compare with the first in terms of the role players' feelings about the resolution?

- What similarities and differences did you see in the two role plays?

- What have you learned about useful behaviors and processes in conflict resolution?

- What behaviors do you plan to use the next time you are involved in an intergroup-conflict situation?

(Fifteen minutes.)

Variations

- Prior to the session, the facilitator may ask the participants to write summaries of intergroup-conflict situations that they have experienced, are experiencing, or have observed. Then these situations may be read in the total group and used as the basis for the choices of role-play situations.

- After Step 10 the facilitator may ask the participants who have only observed so far to choose another situation and role play it. At least one participant should observe each role play and share feedback with the role players afterward.

- The participants can be taught the effective conflict resolution process before they begin the role plays.

- The activity can be used with a group other than two intact work teams.

Submitted by Jason Ollander-Krane and Neil Johnson.

Jason Ollander-Krane is also a managing partner of Ollander-Krane/Johnson. Before forming a partnership with Neil Johnson, he held training and development positions with Wells Fargo Bank, Young and Rubicam, Macy's, and Adia Personnel Services.

Neil Johnson was a managing partner of Ollander-Krane/Johnson, a consulting company specializing in practical, innovative ways to grow, to develop people, to deliver the best products, and to improve sales and service. He designed and delivered programs in management development, selling and service, visioning, and planning for groups and individuals. Organizations also drew on his expertise in facilitating, team building, and other interventions. Neil died of AIDS in June, 1993, after this material was written.

531. Your Book Jacket:
Getting Acquainted

Goals

- To offer the participants an opportunity to become acquainted with one another.

- To offer the participants an opportunity to share personal information with one another in a nonthreatening way.

- To encourage the participants to think creatively.

- To offer a means of increasing participants' self-esteem.

Group Size

Up to thirty participants.

Time Required

Thirty-five minutes to one hour, depending on the size of the group.

Materials

- Assorted colors of 8½" x 11" construction paper, to allow at least one sheet for each participant. (Lighter shades of paper will be most suitable.)

- Felt-tipped pens in assorted colors, to allow at least one pen for each participant.

- A clipboard or other portable writing surface for each participant.

Physical Setting

A room with chairs in which the participants can sit comfortably.

Process

1. The facilitator announces that the participants will have the opportunity to become acquainted with one another in a creative way and gives the following instructions:

   "Please select one sheet of construction paper and a felt-tipped pen. Fold the construction paper in half lengthwise. This will become your book jacket."

   (Five minutes.)

2. The facilitator gives further instructions as follows:

   "Please close your eyes and participate in a visioning activity with me. It is a beautiful day. You are walking down a street in a busy shopping district. You are passing a popular bookstore. In the front window, you see a display of a book that *you* have written on a subject that is very important to you. Please open your eyes now and write down the title of your book on the front cover of your book jacket."

   (Five minutes.)

3. The facilitator continues with the following instructions:

   "Once again, close your eyes and envision yourself in the bookstore, holding your book. You are proud. You turn the book over and you see a photograph of yourself. There is a paragraph under your picture that shares some interesting information about you and praises you highly. What does it say? Please open your eyes, turn over your book jacket, and write down the paragraph that accompanies your photograph."

   (Five minutes.)

4. Each participant is asked to choose a partner. The members of each pair are instructed to read their book jacket information to each other. Partners are encouraged to ask questions and to share information about themselves as openly as they feel comfortable. (Five minutes.)

5. The total group is reassembled. The facilitator gives these instructions:

   "You are to assume the role of editor of your partner's book. Using what you know about your partner, introduce him or her to the group."

   (Five minutes to thirty minutes, depending on the size of the group.)

Pfeiffer & Company

6. After all participants have been introduced, the facilitator leads a discussion of the activity based on questions such as the following:

- What were your reactions to thinking about yourself in this way (as an author)?

- What are your feelings about and reactions to sharing this personal information?

- How did you feel when you were being introduced to the group? How do you account for that?

- How is this similar to other situations where you had to get to know people?

- How can you use what you have learned in getting to know people? Helping others get acquainted? Building trust in a group?

(Ten to fifteen minutes.)

Variations

- Each person may introduce himself or herself to the group.

- Different themes may be highlighted by suggesting in the guided imagery that the participants are visiting a specific section of the bookstore (e.g., business, computer, psychology, history, etc.). The book jackets then will all have the same theme.

- The exercise can be extended by having people describe what kind of book it is, what the chapter headings are, how it would begin, and how it would end.

Submitted by Bonnie Jameson.

Bonnie Jameson is a private consultant who has worked as a designer, trainer, and facilitator in human resource development for the past twenty years. Her special areas of expertise are training for trainers, strategic planning, team building, and leadership. She works with a variety of clients in the for-profit and the nonprofit sectors in the San Francisco area. Currently, Ms. Jameson also teaches courses in strategic planning and building effective organizations in the nonprofit program at California State University in Hayward, California.

532. SEASIDE TOWERS: DESIGNING ONE-TO-ONE TRAINING

Goals

- To encourage the participants to consider and discuss the elements of training design and possible techniques for training, while taking into account individual needs and learning styles.

- To offer the participants an opportunity to practice designing one-to-one training (one trainer, one trainee).

Group Size

Nine to eighteen participants (in three subgroups) who are practicing or prospective trainers.

Time Required

Approximately one hour and forty-five minutes.

Materials

- A copy of the Seaside Towers Background Sheet for each participant.
- A copy of Seaside Towers Task Sheet 1 for each member of subgroup 1.
- A copy of Seaside Towers Task Sheet 2 for each member of subgroup 2.
- A copy of Seaside Towers Task Sheet 3 for each member of subgroup 3.
- A copy of the Seaside Towers Learning-Style Sheet for each participant.
- A pencil for each participant.

The 1995 Annual: Volume 1, Training.
Copyright © 1995 by Pfeiffer & Company, San Diego, CA.

- A newsprint flip chart and a felt-tipped marker.
- Masking tape for posting newsprint.

Physical Setting

A room large enough so that the three subgroups can work without disturbing one another. Movable chairs should be provided as well as tables or portable writing surfaces. Plenty of wall space should be available for posting sheets of newsprint.

Process

1. The facilitator introduces the goals of the activity.

2. The participants are assembled into three subgroups of approximately equal size and are given copies of the Seaside Towers Background Sheet, the Seaside Towers Learning-Style Sheet, and pencils. In addition, each subgroup is given copies of a different task sheet.

3. The participants are told that the background situation is the same for all three subgroups but that each subgroup will be preparing a training program for a different kind of learner. The facilitator allows the participants time to read their handouts and then elicits and answers questions about the task. (Ten to fifteen minutes.)

4. The subgroups are asked to begin the task. The facilitator remains available to answer questions and periodically reminds the subgroups of the remaining time. (Thirty minutes.)

5. After thirty minutes the facilitator calls time and asks the subgroups to take turns describing their assigned trainees and presenting answers to the questions on the task sheets. As each subgroup presents, the facilitator writes a description of the learner on newsprint and records highlights of the answers to questions. After each subgroup has completed its presentation, the facilitator posts that subgroup's newsprint sheet; at the conclusion of this step, all newsprint sheets will be posted side by side, with some space between those belonging to different subgroups. (Thirty minutes.)

6. The facilitator leads a discussion by asking the participants to consider the similarities and differences between the subgroups' training approaches. Care is taken to differentiate between the three sensory styles (visual, auditory, and kinesthetic) and the three attitudes toward learning (dependent, collaborative, and independent). (Ten to fifteen minutes.)

7. The facilitator leads a concluding discussion based on the following questions:

- What was easiest for you in designing the training? Explain. What was most difficult? Explain. How was the difficulty level affected by your own learning style and attitude?

- What have you discovered about sensory styles and their relationship to learning? What have you discovered about attitudes toward learning?

- What past training experiences can you relate to sensory style or attitude toward learning? How did those experiences bear out what you discovered today?

- How will you apply what you have discovered in your future training career?

(Fifteen minutes.)

Variations

- At the conclusion of the activity, the facilitator may invite the participants to form dyads or triads and to take turns helping one another with real problem situations that they are currently experiencing in their work.

- At the conclusion of the activity, each subgroup may be asked to demonstrate with a member of another subgroup how it would train one-on-one for one of the objectives.

Submitted by Lisa Mayocchi, Sharon Harvey, and Ian Croft. The authors wish to thank Dr. Phyllis Tharenou for helpful comments on earlier versions of this activity.

Lisa Mayocchi is a Ph.D. student in organizational psychology in the Department of Psychology at the University of Queensland in Brisbane, Australia. Her research interests lie in the areas of transferable skills, the transfer of training, and sport psychology.

Sharon Harvey, M.B.A., is a marketing information manager with Incitec Ltd. in Brisbane. Her work involves market research and market analysis, and she is particularly interested in the development of individual employees to enhance team performance.

Ian Croft, M.B.A., is a teacher with the Queensland Department of Education. His recent studies have focused on human resource issues with particular emphasis on their relevance to education.

SEASIDE TOWERS BACKGROUND SHEET

The Situation

You are a member of a human resource development firm in a resort town. A recently opened local hotel, the Seaside Towers, has just contracted with your firm to provide training on procedures for hotel personnel to follow in the event of a fire.

Although your firm has provided training for many clients on a number of topics, you and the other staff members are not familiar with the steps that must be taken in the event of a fire in a facility such as a hotel. Consequently, the management of your firm has called a meeting to discuss what needs to be done to plan the training for Seaside.

Training Objectives

Prior to this meeting, the management of your firm conducted a task analysis as well as an assessment of the trainees' current knowledge and concluded that the trainees must learn how to do the following:

- Explain the relationship between fuel, heat, and oxygen;
- Demonstrate the use of a real fire extinguisher in a classroom setting with 90-percent accuracy;
- Explain what needs to be done to act safely in the hazardous environment associated with a fire; and
- Explain the procedures to follow in the event of a fire (for example, whom to contact and how to ensure the safety of guests).

Your opinion is that one-to-one training is the most appropriate means of training because hotel-staffing requirements allow only one person to be released from regular duties for training at any one time.

Seaside Towers Task Sheet 1

Your Trainee

Your trainee is *Chris,* whose preferred sensory style is *visual.* In addition, Chris is a *dependent* learner.

Questions to Answer

Your subgroup will be asked to present answers as well as rationales to answers to the following questions:

1. What resources will you use to plan and conduct the training? Which people/experts will you consult?

2. What learning activities will you employ?

3. What will be the major steps of the training event, and in what sequence should these steps be taken?

4. What other arrangements will you make?

5. What constraints might you have to operate within? How will you plan for and deal with these constraints?

6. How will you evaluate the effectiveness of your training?

SEASIDE TOWERS TASK SHEET 2

Your Trainee

Your trainee is *Lee,* whose preferred sensory style is *auditory.* In addition, Lee is a *collaborative* learner.

Questions to Answer

Your subgroup will be asked to present answers as well as rationales for answers to the following questions:

1. What resources will you use to plan and conduct the training? Which people/experts will you consult?

2. What learning activities will you employ?

3. What will be the major steps of the training event, and in what sequence should these steps be taken?

4. What other arrangements will you make?

5. What constraints might you have to operate within? How will you plan for and deal with these constraints?

6. How will you evaluate the effectiveness of your training?

The 1995 Annual: Volume 1, Training.
Copyright © 1995 by Pfeiffer & Company, San Diego, CA.

SEASIDE TOWERS TASK SHEET 3

Your Trainee

Your trainee is *Terry,* whose preferred sensory style is *kinesthetic.* In addition, Terry is an *independent* learner.

Questions to Answer

1. What resources will you use to plan and conduct the training? Which people/experts will you consult? Why?

2. What learning activities will you employ? Why?

3. What will be the major steps of the training event?

4. What other arrangements will you make?

5. What constraints might you have to operate within? How will you plan for and deal with these constraints?

6. How will you evaluate the effectiveness of your training?

SEASIDE TOWERS LEARNING-STYLE SHEET

Visual, Auditory, and Kinesthetic Learners[1]

Visual learners should be provided continually with visual learning aids such as posters, booklets, memory maps, and charts. They like to see demonstrations, diagrams, slides, and so on while they are learning.

Auditory learners should be allowed to hear material (for example, poster content read aloud, audiotapes, or guided imagery). They like verbal instructions, discussions, and lectures while they are learning.

Kinesthetic learners prefer activities that involve movement and hands-on experience. They favor direct involvement in activities, such as role playing.

Dependent, Independent, and Collaborative Learners[2]

Dependent learners tend to display a "teach-me" attitude toward learning. They expect trainers to assume full responsibility for any learning that occurs. Often they are eager to learn but are likely to assume that they cannot do so without help. These learners are most productive in structured learning environments and often require a great deal of support and encouragement to move into more collaborative and/or independent learning situations.

Collaborative learners expect to share responsibility for learning and for establishing learning objectives and course content. They value participation, interaction, teamwork, and the knowledge and expertise of their peers. They may feel uncomfortable in highly structured learning environments and at times may have difficulty recognizing trainers' expertise in designing independent learning projects and in facilitating the learning process.

Independent learners expect to set and achieve their own learning goals. They perceive trainers as holders of the knowledge and expertise that will help them to achieve their personal goals. Independent learners are comfortable working alone and require only minimal contact with others. The independent style of learning is highly active and can be expressed in the phrase "Help me to learn to do it myself."

---

[1] Lengthier descriptions of sensory styles appear in *Accelerated Learning* (4th ed.) by C. Rose, 1989, Aylesbury, Buckinghamshire, England: Accelerated Learning Systems.

[2] These descriptions of learning attitudes have been condensed from *Presentation and Evaluation Skills in Human Resource Development* (UATT Series, Vol. 7) by J.W. Pfeiffer and A.C. Ballew, 1988, San Diego, CA: Pfeiffer & Company.

Introduction
to the Inventories, Questionnaires, and Surveys Section

Instrumented survey-feedback tools give participants opportunities to develop an understanding of the theories involved in the dynamics of their own group situations—understanding that will increase their involvement. Instruments allow the facilitator of a small group to focus the energies and time of the participants on the most appropriate material and also to direct, to some extent, the matters that are dealt with in a session. In this way, the facilitator can ensure that the issues worked on are crucial, existing ones, rather than the less important ones that the members may introduce to avoid grappling with the more uncomfortable issues.

The contents of the Inventories, Questionnaires, and Surveys section are provided for training and development purposes. These instruments are not intended for in-depth personal growth, psychodiagnostic, or therapeutic work. Instead, they are intended for use in training groups; for demonstration purposes; to generate data for training or organization development sessions; and for other group applications in which the trainer, consultant, or facilitator helps respondents to use the data generated by an instrument for achieving some form of progress.

Each instrument includes the theory necessary for understanding, presenting, and using it. All interpretive information, scales or inventory forms, and scoring sheets are also provided for each instrument. In addition, Pfeiffer & Company publishes all of the reliability and validity data contributed by the authors of instruments; if readers want additional information on reliability and validity, they are encouraged to contact instrument authors directly. (Authors' addresses and telephone numbers appear in the Contributors list that follows the Presentation and Discussion Resources section.)

The 1995 Annual: Volume 1, Training includes three assessment tools, in the following categories:

Individual Development

Life-Orientation Inventory, by Udai Pareek (page 141)

Communication

Cross-Cultural Interactive Preference Profile, by Morris Graham and Dwight Miller (page 111)

Groups and Teams

Diversity Awareness Assessment, by David P. Tulin (page 131)

Other assessment tools that address certain goals can be located by using our comprehensive *Reference Guide to Handbooks and Annuals*. This book, which is updated regularly, indexes all of the *Annuals* and all of the *Handbooks of Structured Experiences* that we have published to date. With each revision, the *Reference Guide* becomes a complete, up-to-date, and easy-to-use resource for selecting appropriate materials from *all* of the *Annuals* and *Handbooks*.

CROSS-CULTURAL INTERACTIVE PREFERENCE PROFILE

Morris Graham and Dwight Miller

Abstract: Many people encounter problems interacting in environments that are culturally different from their own. Everyone has preferences regarding inter-personal interactions, and these may vary from culture to culture as well as from individual to individual.

One important dimension of culture is *context,* which ranges from *high context* (collectivism) to *low context* (individualism). The Cross-Cultural Interactive Preference (CCIP) Profile measures an individual's preferences for level of context as well as his or her ability to interact effectively across contexts. This pro-file comprises the following factors: socialization of information, socialization of people, spatial orienta-tion, and time orientation. As a result of understand-ing his or her own preferences, a person can become more aware of the role that context plays in individual and group interactions.

Most people do not do really well when interacting in an environment that is foreign to their own or with people of cultural preferences different from their own. This is particularly true within cross-cultural or cross-functional groups. Preferences regarding interpersonal interactions, group interactions, and information may vary from one culture to another, just as they also vary from one individual to another, regardless of cultural origin. People's interactive preferences need to be understood in order to facilitate productive group work. Such understanding can help to reduce potential interpersonal conflicts and can increase group effectiveness.

In cross-cultural or cross-functional group settings, what we can learn about ourselves through others is as important as what we can learn about others and their cultures. The ways in which we feel, think, and behave can be checked in terms of how others perceive and interact with us. Things take on new meanings in the context of other cultural orientations. Moreover, things that we may consider to be uniquely individual about our "selves" are actually shaped by our culture, which determines, to a large extent, how we respond in different situations.

The Cross-Cultural Interactive Preference Profile (CCIP Profile) identifies how the respondents would prefer to interact in group activities or in situations in which more than one cultural orientation is involved.

Definitions of Terms

Understanding any subject area requires a basic working vocabulary. In the cross-cultural field, this vocabulary has grown with the advance of research. However, only the essential terms are defined here, for the purpose of interpreting the CCIP Profile.

Assimilate: To become absorbed into the cultural traditions of another ethnic population or group.

Context: The information that surrounds an event and is inextricably bound up with the meaning of the event. The elements that combine to produce a given meaning—events and context—vary in proportion from culture to culture. The cultures of the world can be compared on a scale from low context to high context (Hall & Hall, 1990).

Cross-Cultural Activities: Activities that involve more than one cultural set, viewpoint, or environment. Such activities deal with an individual's personal and cultural self-awareness, other-awareness, intercultural communication barriers, and interaction skills (Brislin, 1990).

Culture: A collection of many beliefs, values, perspectives, behaviors, activities, institutions, and learned patterns of communication largely shared in common by a group of people.

High-Context Message: Communication in which the vast majority of the information is either internalized in the individual or the physical context of the situation. Very little is in the explicit transmission or coding of the message (Hall, 1977; Hall & Hall, 1990).

Judgment: The process of forming conclusions about what has been perceived by an individual.

Low-Context Message: Communication in which the mass of information is in the explicit coding of the message and not resident within the individuals involved or within the situation or context (Hall, 1977).

Microculture: A subculture or new culture formed by the interaction of two or more major cultures such as business organizations, nations, or persons. A formulation of beliefs, behaviors, values, characteristics, patterns of communication, etc., shared by a specific group of people, that originates from diverse, major cultural groupings (Fontaine, 1989).

Multicultural Individual: An individual who has assimilated understanding, precepts, knowledge, and characteristics of more than his or her own native culture by experiencing microcultural activities of cross-cultural groups. Adler (1986) notes that members of multicultural groups should recognize and integrate all the cultures represented.

Multiculturalism: Situations in which people from more than one culture (and frequently more than one country) interact regularly, thus forming a number of perspectives, approaches, and—in the case of businesses—business methods (Adler, 1986).

Personality: The result of conditioning by culture; the total of the individual's characteristic reactions to his or her environment.

Predisposition: The condition of being inclined beforehand or having a susceptibility to act or react in a particular way.

Conceptual Background: Low-Context and High-Context Orientations

Theorists have identified a major dimension of cultural variability, called "context" (Chinese Culture Connection, 1987; Hall, 1977; Hall & Hall, 1990;

Hofstede, 1984; Kluckhohn & Strodtbeck, 1961; Marsella, DeVos, & Hsu, 1985; Triandis, 1988). The two basic dimensions of are low context (individualism) and high context (collectivism).

Low-Context Cultures (Individualism)

Low-context, or "individualistic," people and cultures place emphasis on individualism and individual goals, facts, the management of time, nonverbal communication, privacy, and compartmentalization.

The cultural norms associated with low context, which dominate most North American and Northern European societies, are essentially task-oriented, focusing on data to provide the answers to living well. Progress is measured in tangibles. Goals are action-oriented and geared to produce short-term material profits. The driving force of a low-context culture is work, which is the usual context in which a person is honored. Societies are structured to honor individuals who succeed financially. Emotions are suspect and considered inappropriate in most social and work settings.

> *The driving force of a low-context culture is work.*

Low-context people are highly individualistic, assertive, directive, dominating, results-oriented, independent, strong-willed, competitive, quick to make decisions, impatient, time-conscious, solution-oriented, control-seeking, well-organized, and self-contained. The individual has a high need to be recognized for his or her performance.

Individualistic social skills include meeting people quickly, putting them at ease, finding topics of conversation that others can discuss readily, being interesting so that the others will have memories of the interaction six months later, and so forth. These skills are useful, as they allow people to obtain information from others, central to the pursuit of individual goals (Brislin, 1993).

In a group setting, low-context individuals need less time to develop new, progressive programs that can be changed easily and quickly. However, these individuals can create less cohesion and stability in the group. Also, they are less committed to group agreements or planned actions.

In low-context cultures, when there is a conflict between an individual's goals and those of a valued group (i.e., coworkers), consideration of the individual's goals is of major importance. Individualists report (Brislin, 1993) that they would feel stifled if they were surrounded by others. There would be too many people whose opinions would have to be considered before an individualist could act in the pursuit of his or her goals. Individualists find that clearing their plans with others interferes too much with their desire "to do their own thing."

High-Context Cultures (Collectivism)

High-context, or "collectivistic," individuals and cultures place emphasis on relationships, group goals, the process and surrounding circumstances, time as natural progression, verbal communication, communal space, and inter-relationships.

High-context cultural norms are primarily group-oriented, i.e., honoring the relationships of their cultural group before that of an "out-group," such as a university, company, or country. Family and community ties are strong; feelings and emotions are valued and encouraged to be expressed; religious and spiritual beliefs are deep.

In a high-context culture, behavior is viewed in a complex way. People look beyond the obvious to note nuances in meaning, nonverbal communication cues, and the status of others *in context*. In general, Asian cultural orientations are high context.

Personal characteristics include being indirect, highly affiliative, team-oriented, systematic, steady, quiet, patient, loyal, dependable, informal, servicing, sharing, slow in making decisions, respectful, and good listeners. A longer amount of time is needed for individuals to become acquainted with and trusting of one another; after that, communication is fast. The culture is rooted in the past; it is a slow-to-change, highly stable, unified group.

Collectivists feel comfortable with the constant psychological presence of a group. Important collective social attributes are loyalty to the group, cooperation, contributing to the group without the expectation of immediate reciprocity, and public modesty about one's abilities (Triandis, 1988). People are more likely to downplay their own goals in favor of the goals of the valued group. Individuals are more committed to group agreements and planned actions.

Contextual Factors

The factors or dimensions of context are time and space (Hall, 1977; Hall & Hall, 1990). These factors can be considered across all cultures; they are not specific to one culture or another or have meaning in and of themselves. Hall notes the importance of these factors as information is disseminated and acted on.

Hall uses the terms "monochronic" and "polychronic" to describe the individual orientations to time. In monochronic time, one pays attention to and does only one thing at a time. Events, functions, people, communication, and information flow are compartmentalized. In monochronic cultures, people are governed by time and work and they communicate in a linear fashion. In polychronic time, many things may happen or receive attention at the same time. In polychronic cultures, there is great involvement with people and events. People take precedence over time and schedules, and there is an emphasis on completing human transactions.

Monochronic cultures are basically low-context cultures that control and restrict information flow and communication. Polychronic cultures are basically high-context cultures in which information flows freely among all participants. Because the information is available to all, one is expected to use intuition and to understand automatically.

The purpose of meetings and communication in low-context cultures is to pass and/or determine information in order to evaluate and make decisions. In high-context cultures, the purpose of meetings is to reach consensus about what is already known. The two processes are mutually exclusive in that in the low context, meaning is derived primarily from the coding of the messages. In the high context, the individuals already have the information or message within them. Hall and Hall (1990, p. 19) strongly emphasize the fact that "one must always be contexted to the local time systems" when working across cultures.

> *Context will largely determine the message that a person receives.*

Spatial changes influence and often give definition to communications and human interaction even to the extent of overriding the spoken word. Spatial cues are perceived by all of the senses. Some cultures may attune more to the auditory, some to kinesthetic, others to visual, and so on. Each individual is surrounded by invisible boundaries of personal space or territories. These often communicate ownership or power when linked to physical location. With low-context monochronic societies and individuals, personal space is private, controlled, and often large. In contrast, in high-context polychronic societies or individuals, space is often shared with subordinates and centralized or shared in an information network. Time and space are often closely linked in that access to individuals is often dictated by both location and timing. An individual's availability is often determined by how well he or she is screened or separated from others.

Context and Communication

In his book, *Beyond Culture,* Hall (1977) identifies the critical need for individuals to transcend cultural barriers. He challenges us to "...recognize and accept the multiple hidden dimensions of unconscious culture..." (p. 2), because each culture has its own hidden or unconscious dimensions. In analyzing communication factors, Hall notes that it is impossible to know the meaning of a communication without knowing the context. Barker (1968) established that as the ecology or environment changed, so did people's responses.

With regard to context in relation to meaning, Hall (1977) states that context will largely determine the message that a person receives. Hall defines the collectivistic, high-context (HC) message or communication as one in which the vast majority of the information is either internalized in the individual or in the physical context of the situation. Very little is in the explicit transmission or coding of the message. With the individualistic, low-context (LC) message, the mass of information is in the explicit coding of the message, not within the individual or the situation (context).

Individuals perform the critically important function of correcting for distortions or omissions in the messages they receive. The key to being effective in communicating across cultures is in knowing the degree of information—context—that must be supplied and in the correct reading of another individual's verbal *and* nonverbal behavior. The context—the information surrounding an event that gives it meaning—varies from culture to culture and is often the determining factor in whether or not individuals from different cultures will communicate effectively, reach understanding, and make decisions. The integration of both verbal message and context is the basis of effective communication (Hall, 1977; Hall & Hall, 1990).

THE PROFILE

High versus low context, individualism versus collectivism, and the factors of time and space are not the only dimensions by which culture can be analyzed. However, they are ways in which a determination can be made as to how to communicate and work with individuals, regardless of their cultural orientations. Although many comparisons of major ethnic and national groups have been made based on contextual needs and decision-making processes, few, if any, have been developed to measure individual responses. The Cross-Cultural Interactive Preference Profile (CCIP Profile) was developed to reveal an individual's preferences in terms of contextual needs and socialization in interactive, group-decision-making processes so that effective communication, facilitation, and training designs could be established.

Development

The profile items were developed from a review of the literature and were given to seven experts who had extensive knowledge and experience in cross-cultural environmental learning and group interaction. A conceptual review was completed first. To establish content validity on revisions, a Delphi panel was asked to review each of the profile items for appropriateness and inclusion. This panel was selected on the basis of working experience in highly cross-cultural learning environments and experience in designing either assessment tools or training materials that had been applied in that environment. Panel members also had worked as consultants or employees in business and industry. They reviewed items based on appropriateness to the culturally defined categories, readability, comprehension, and the exclusion of culturally charged contextual items. Individual reviews and further revisions continued until at least 75 percent of panel members agreed on each of the forty-eight retained items.

The profile was pilot tested with a culturally mixed group of university students, and feedback was solicited about the profile through focus groups and an interview process. Particular attention was paid to comprehensibility of the language. Minor adjustments were made before administering the CCIP Profile to 512 freshmen and sophomore students (247 males and 265 females) at Brigham Young University-Hawaii, where fifty cultural orientations were represented. Approximately 20 percent of the students were from the mainland United States and other (predominantly European) Western cultural mixes, 25 percent were from Hawaii, 25 percent were from the South Pacific, 25 percent were from the Asian-rim countries, and the remainder were from other parts of the world. It was observed that most foreign students, after their arrival on campus, would develop and retain socialization patterns that maintained close ties to their own cultural groups through culture-based clubs and organizations. Thus, the majority of the students surveyed were close to their native orientations.

The CCIP Profile is intended for use with individuals who are involved in cross-cultural activities that result in the development of knowledge and skills. The profile is designed to foster awareness of, and sensitivity to, contextual orientation that affect interactive behavior in culturally diverse groups.

Validity

The content validity of the profile was assured through the implementation of the literature review, the iterative Delphi panel, and interviews during the pilot-testing stages.

Construct validity was determined by assessing the relationship of test items with cultural groups through the use of factor analysis and multidiscriminant analysis. The profile employs a Likert scale, which resulted in a single factor or construct when factor analysis was applied. Factor loadings were above a level of .45. To assure validity, more than ten respondents per item were utilized. Item analysis utilizing two-tail probability showed a *p*-value .001 on all items.

Overall validity was based on the strength of the factor-1 loadings and the significance levels of the individual items. However, it is noted that there are some weaknesses to be dealt with through a continued analysis with additional populations.

Reliability

There are no current tests or standards with which to compare the results of the profile administration. A coefficient of internal consistency was determined utilizing a single-test administration. Cronbach's Coefficient Alpha was used to test reliability, as the profile relies on a nondichotomous, six-level Likert scale to circumvent a neutral or nonresponse, and a method of rational equivalence could not be used. Reliability coefficients (alphas) were: .49 in seven of the eight factor groupings, with the eighth at .34.

Suggested Use

The CCIP Profile can be used in various aspects of group decision making, cross-cultural conflict resolution, training and development, and team development in diverse work and educational settings. It is particularly useful as a clarification tool with newly organized groups or teams. Facilitators can be assured that finding out about one's own and others' preferences is a releasing experience, not a restricting one, as may be feared. Finding out about cultural preferences frees group members to recognize their own natural predispositions and to respect and learn how to effectively interact with the differences in the group with a minimum of conflict. Groups can become less polar or fragmented and more multiculturally sensitive and unified in their interactions.

References

Adler, N.J. (1986). In D.A. Ricks (Ed.), *International dimensions of organizational behavior* (The Kent International Business Series). Boston, MA: Kent Publishing.

Barker, R.G. (1968). *Ecological psychology.* Stanford, CA: Stanford University Press.

Brislin, R. (1993). *Understanding culture's influence on behavior.* Fort Worth, TX: Harcourt Brace College.

Brislin, R.W. (Ed.). (1990). *Applied cross-cultural psychology* (Cross-Cultural Research and Methodology Series No. 14). Newbury Park, CA: Sage.

Chinese Culture Connection. (1987). Chinese values and the search for culture-free dimensions of culture. *Journal of Cross-Cultural Psychology, 18,* 143-164.

Fontaine, G. (1989). *Managing international assignments.* Englewood Cliffs, NJ: Prentice Hall.

Hall, E.T. (1977). *Beyond culture.* Garden City, NY: Anchor Press/Doubleday.

Hall, E.T., & Hall, M.R. (1990). *Understanding cultural differences.* Yarmouth, ME: Intercultural Press.

Hofstede, G. (1984). *Culture's consequences: International differences in work-related values.* Newbury Park, CA: Sage.

Kluckhohn, F., & Strodtbeck, F. (1961). *Variations in value orientations.* New York: Row, Peterson.

Marsella, A.J., DeVos, G., & Hsu, F.L.K (Eds.). (1985). *Culture and self: Asian and Western perspectives.* New York: Tavistock.

Triandis, H.C. (1988). Collectivism vs. individualism: A reconceptualization of a basic concept in cross-cultural psychology. In G. Verma & C. Bagley (Eds.), *Cross-cultural studies of personality, attitudes and cognition* (pp. 60-95). London: Macmillan.

Triandis, H.C. (1990). Cross-cultural studies of individualism-collectivism. In J. Berman (Ed.), *Nebraska Symposium on Motivation 1989* (Vol. 35, pp. 41-53). Lincoln, NE: University of Nebraska Press.

Morris Graham, Ph.D., is a professor of organizational psychology and director of the Organizational Development program at Brigham Young University-Hawaii. He has served as a national director with the American Society of Training and Development and as a manager of the International Federation of Training and Development Organisations (London). Dr. Graham has published numerous articles and is the author of The Horizontal Revolution: Reengineering Your Organization Through Teams *(Jossey-Bass Publishers, 1994). He consults with organizations nationally and internationally on how to implement high-performance work systems in multicultural settings.*

Dwight Miller, Ed.D., is an associate professor and coordinator of systems development and network management for academic support at Brigham Young University-Hawaii. He has consulted in the field of leadership and group analysis. Dr. Miller has produced numerous video and training materials for educational and public institutions.

Cross-Cultural Interactive Preferences Profile

Morris Graham and Dwight Miller

There are no right or wrong answers on this questionnaire. The answers will be useful only if you respond honestly and candidly. By doing this, you will help us to better understand the ways in which you prefer to interact within a group where there is more than one culture represented.

Instructions: The following items describe how you might interact within a work or problem-solving group. Respond to each item by filling in the circle that best describes your preference, that is, how strongly you agree or disagree with the statement. This should take about fifteen minutes.

Example:

You would mark your questionnaire

If you strongly agreed with this statement:

↓

It's O.K. for new situations or ideas
to be presented to the group for a decision
even if some details are not included.

You would mark your questionnaire

If you disagreed with this statement:

↓

I would let members do their own
work the way they think best.

SD = Strongly Disagree   MA = Mildly Agree
D = Disagree   A = Agree
MD = Mildly Disagree   SA = Strongly Agree

The 1995 Annual: Volume 1, Training.
Copyright © 1995 by Pfeiffer & Company, San Diego, CA.

SD D MD MA A SA   1. I need the leader of the group to explain the details before I can make a decision.

SD D MD MA A SA   2. I work best when we share information and then reach consensus as a group.

SD D MD MA A SA   3. Information should be held in common and not controlled by specific individuals or parts of the group.

SD D MD MA A SA   4. It is better to quietly acknowledge that a person may be incorrect or needs to change rather than to openly confront him/her in the group.

SD D MD MA A SA   5. It is best for all decisions to be approved by the whole group.

SD D MD MA A SA   6. Experts within a group should be allowed to make decisions for the group.

SD D MD MA A SA   7. Getting the details of needed information is more important than knowing who provided them.

SD D MD MA A SA   8. I am impatient when someone tries to explain something I already know.

SD D MD MA A SA   9. Individuals within a group do not need to share the information they have with the rest of the group until it is absolutely necessary.

SD D MD MA A SA   10. It is not important that all members of a group contribute ideas.

SD D MD MA A SA   11. I would compromise with others in order to maintain harmony in the group.

SD D MD MA A SA   12. I would expect the team leader to direct members away from problems or issues that would upset the balance of the group.

SD D MD MA A SA   13. I would trust the group members and support their shared interests even if I do not agree with them.

SD D MD MA A SA   14. I would use the utmost diplomacy in order not to embarrass anyone while working through problems in the group.

SD D MD MA A SA   15. Once a commitment has the group's approval, it is expected to be honored.

(SD) (D) (MD) (MA) (A) (SA) 16. I would decide on my own what should be done and how it should be done.

(SD) (D) (MD) (MA) (A) (SA) 17. I would direct others toward getting results as soon as possible.

(SD) (D) (MD) (MA) (A) (SA) 18. I would directly confront problems or conflicts between individuals in the group.

(SD) (D) (MD) (MA) (A) (SA) 19. I would say what I thought, even though it may hurt others' feelings.

(SD) (D) (MD) (MA) (A) (SA) 20. I would want outstanding individual performers in group activities rewarded more than those who did not contribute as much.

(SD) (D) (MD) (MA) (A) (SA) 21. I don't like doing work on my own or being separate from the group.

(SD) (D) (MD) (MA) (A) (SA) 22. I feel uncomfortable when there are individuals in the group who remain distant and don't interact with the group.

(SD) (D) (MD) (MA) (A) (SA) 23. In a group meeting, it is important that we stay close together.

(SD) (D) (MD) (MA) (A) (SA) 24. It is best to have the leader in a centralized location where all members of the group can interact with him or her.

(SD) (D) (MD) (MA) (A) (SA) 25. The best way to work in a group is to stay together in the same room until agreement is reached.

(SD) (D) (MD) (MA) (A) (SA) 26. I don't want to be interrupted when I'm working on or thinking about a problem.

(SD) (D) (MD) (MA) (A) (SA) 27. I need to be away from the group in order to think and make a decision.

(SD) (D) (MD) (MA) (A) (SA) 28. I prefer to work alone until I am ready to get with the group.

(SD) (D) (MD) (MA) (A) (SA) 29. The leader of a group or organization needs to be separate but where I can go to him or her when I need to.

(SD) (D) (MD) (MA) (A) (SA) 30. When working in a group, I prefer to work with individuals who think as I do.

(SD) (D) (MD) (MA) (A) (SA) 31. I would desire lots of time and flexibility to accommodate the different personalities in the group.

(SD) (D) (MD) (MA) (A) (SA) 32. If there were disagreement in the group, I would be patient while others worked through and resolved conflicts before proceeding.

(SD) (D) (MD) (MA) (A) (SA) 33. It is more important to take the time needed to develop or share ideas before making a decision than it is to meet deadlines.

(SD) (D) (MD) (MA) (A) (SA) 34. It is O.K. to stop a group discussion and take a break whenever needed.

(SD) (D) (MD) (MA) (A) (SA) 35. Plans should always be open to change.

(SD) (D) (MD) (MA) (A) (SA) 36. A group should not stop working or discussing until a solution is found or a decision is made.

(SD) (D) (MD) (MA) (A) (SA) 37. I would not tolerate postponements.

(SD) (D) (MD) (MA) (A) (SA) 38. It is very important that a schedule be maintained.

(SD) (D) (MD) (MA) (A) (SA) 39. The group should deal with only one thing at a time until a decision is made.

(SD) (D) (MD) (MA) (A) (SA) 40. When the group has finished its work, it is best to move on and form new relationships.

CCIP Profile Scoring Sheet

Instructions: Convert each rating that you gave to a profile item to a number, as shown, and place that number in the appropriate spaces on this sheet.

SD=0   D=1   MD=2   MA=3   A=4   SA=5

Factor	Subscores		
Socialization of Information	Item — Highly Shared Flow		Item — Controlled Flow
	1. _____		6. _____
	2. _____		7. _____
	3. _____		8. _____
	4. _____		9. _____
	5. _____		10. _____
	Total _____		Total _____
Socialization of People	Item — Collectivist		Item — Individualist
	11. _____		16. _____
	12. _____		17. _____
	13. _____		18. _____
	14. _____		19. _____
	15. _____		20. _____
	Total _____		Total _____
Spatial Orientation	Item — Shared/Central		Item — Personalized
	21. _____		26. _____
	22. _____		27. _____
	23. _____		28. _____
	24. _____		29. _____
	25. _____		30. _____
	Total _____		Total _____
Time Orientation	Item — Polychronic		Item — Monochronic
	31. _____		36. _____
	32. _____		37. _____
	33. _____		38. _____
	34. _____		39. _____
	35. _____		40. _____
	Total _____		Total _____

Place the *total scores* in the appropriate boxes on the following sheet.

The 1995 Annual: Volume 1, Training.
Copyright © 1995 by Pfeiffer & Company, San Diego, CA.

CCIP Profile Interpretation Graph

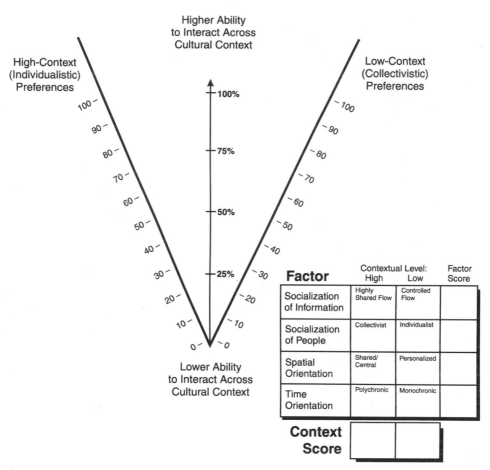

Higher Ability to Interact Across Cultural Context

High-Context (Individualistic) Preferences

Low-Context (Collectivistic) Preferences

100%

75%

50%

25%

Lower Ability to Interact Across Cultural Context

Factor	Contextual Level: High	Low	Factor Score
Socialization of Information	Highly Shared Flow	Controlled Flow	
Socialization of People	Collectivist	Individualist	
Spatial Orientation	Shared/ Central	Personalized	
Time Orientation	Polychronic	Monochronic	
Context Score			

Instructions:

1. Place the total scores from the CCIP Profile Scoring Sheet in the Factor boxes above.
2. Sum each row across to determine the Factor Score. Sum each column down to determine the Context Score.
3. Plot the "contextual level scores" on the graph, with the high-context score on the left axis and the low-context score on the right axis. Draw a line between the two plotted points.

The 1995 Annual: Volume 1, Training.
Copyright © 1995 by Pfeiffer & Company, San Diego, CA.

CCIP Profile Interpretation Sheet

Background

As individuals develop within their cultures and in interactions with others, they form preferences about various aspects of interpersonal interactions. Many of these preferences have been identified in terms of what is called "context." Two basic contexts are "individualistic" and "collectivistic." The context in which one is interacting affects how one relates to others, communicates, interprets information, and so on.

Individualistic

Individualistic people and cultures focus on individual goals, tasks, facts, solutions, time management, and privacy. Individualists are assertive, directive, controlling, results-oriented, independent, strong-willed, competitive, quick to make decisions, impatient, organized, self-contained, and have a high need to be recognized for their performance. Goals are action-oriented to produce short-term material profits, and financial success is esteemed. Emotions are considered inappropriate in most social and work settings.

Individualists tend to have a monochronic time focus. One pays attention to and does only one thing at a time. Events, functions, people, communication, and information flow are compartmentalized.

Individualistic communication is "low context," which means that interactions are linear and specific and do not carry a lot of cultural "context" within them. Meaning is derived primarily from the coding of the message. Social skills include meeting people quickly, finding topics of conversation that others can discuss readily, being interesting so that the others will have memories of the interaction six months later, and obtaining information from others in pursuit of individual goals (Brislin, 1993).

Individualists' plans are progressive and can be changed quickly. However, such individuals can create less cohesion and stability in a group. They are less committed to group agreements, and when there is a conflict between an individual's goals and those of the group, the individual's goals are of major importance. Individualists do not like to have to consider the opinions of others before they act. Clearing their plans with others interferes too much with their desire "to do their own thing" (Brislin, 1993).

Collectivistic

Collectivistic individuals and cultures place emphasis on relationships, group goals, the process and surrounding circumstances, time as natural progression, verbal communication, communal space, and interrelationships. Cultural norms are primarily group oriented. Family and community ties are strong; expression of feelings is valued and encouraged; religious and spiritual beliefs are deep. These mutual understandings and beliefs supply the "high context" of this orientation.

In such a culture, behavior is viewed in a complex way. People look beyond the obvious to note nuances in meaning, nonverbal communication cues, and the status of others in the context of a shared history and understanding. Thus, language need not be as specific; relationships are part of the message. Because the information is available to all, one is expected to use intuition and to understand automatically.

Personal characteristics include being: indirect, affiliative, informal, team-oriented, loyal, systematic, quiet, patient, dependable, cooperative, sharing, slow in making decisions, respectful, a good listener, contributing to the group without the expectation of immediate reciprocity, and public modesty about one's abilities (Triandis, 1990). A longer amount of time is needed for individuals to become acquainted with and trusting of one another; after that, communication is fast. The culture is rooted in the past; it is slow-to-change, highly stable, unified.

People are more likely to downplay their own goals in favor of the goals of the group, and individuals are more committed to group agreements.

Collectivists tend to have a polychronic time focus. Many things may happen or receive attention at the same time. There is great involvement with people and events. People take precedence over time and schedules, and there is an emphasis on completing human transactions.

Hall (1977) notes that it is impossible to know the meaning of a communication without knowing the context. Context largely determines what one pays attention to or does not pay attention to. The information surrounding an event that gives it meaning varies from culture to culture. The key to being effective in communicating across cultures is in knowing the degree of information—context—that must be supplied and in the correct reading of another individual's verbal *and* nonverbal behavior.

Individual Application

People who score high on one side of the CCIP Profile Interpretation Graph and low on the opposite side (a steeply sloped profile) may interact well with those who have profiles similar to theirs, but not with others.

People whose scores are relatively high on both sides of the graph (a flat profile) probably have little difficulty in interacting within groups in which there are varying levels of contextual requirements. These people are better able to move between situations and/or groups with ease, to be more flexible and adaptable in interpretation and decision-making situations, and to be more responsive in learning and decision making. The higher the flat profile, the greater the flexibility.

The factor scores represent relative levels in each of the factor preference areas. Where flexibility and adaptability problems exist, low scores may indicate which orientation or requirement may be responsible. Sub scores will indicate the dominance of the characteristic. The differences between sub scores indicate level of flexibility for a characteristic (higher differences represent higher flexibility). In general, low scores represent a potential difficulty in interacting across contextual boundaries.

Note: Language, religion, philosophical, and other communication or social barriers are not included in this profile.

References

Brislin, R. (1993). *Understanding culture's influence on behavior.* Fort Worth, TX: Harcourt Brace College.

Hall, E.T. (1977). *Beyond culture.* Garden City, NY: Anchor Press/Doubleday.

Triandis, H.C. (1990). Cross-cultural studies of individualism-collectivism. In J. Berman (Ed.), *Nebraska Symposium on Motivation 1989* (Vol. 35, pp. 41-53). Lincoln, NE: University of Nebraska Press.

DIVERSITY AWARENESS ASSESSMENT

David P. Tulin

Abstract: Many organizations begin diversity training without sufficient knowledge of preexisting conditions. Diversity training in particular can be volatile if approached incorrectly. Facilitators need tools that assist them in approaching the topic of diversity in a nonthreatening manner, thereby allowing people to feel more comfortable talking about diversity issues.

This self-assessment, an excerpt of a longer assessment, provides a quick measure of respondents' levels of knowledge of general and business-related multicultural information. Using this type of assessment demonstrates that everyone has more to learn about diversity and provides an opportunity for people to ask diversity-related questions in a safe environment.

Diversity-awareness tools have three general purposes: (1) to get people thinking about diversity issues, (2) to challenge implicit assumptions and biases that might otherwise go unexamined, and (3) to consider other points of view from the perspective of other cultures. Organizations today need tools with which to explore both their willingness and their skills in terms of functioning effectively in a multicultural context.

The Diversity Awareness Assessment[1] has been designed as a diversity-awareness tool. This self-assessment measures respondents' levels of knowledge of general and business-related multicultural information. Although organized in the form of multiple-choice questions, this assessment is not a "test." It purposely is anonymous so that respondents can recognize their own knowledge and needs for improvement with minimal concerns about being embarrassed or defensive.

DESCRIPTION OF THE INSTRUMENT

The Diversity Awareness Assessment consists of twenty multiple-choice questions. Respondents circle the answers they believe to be correct. The assessment will take approximately ten to fifteen minutes to complete. Respondents should be assured beforehand that no one is expected to know all of the answers. Rather, the very nature of the field of diversity means that there is no end to the challenge of increasing knowledge and competencies. The results are intended to evoke discussion among the respondents rather than teach particular facts. The assessment therefore has face validity only.

After all respondents have finished completing the assessment, the facilitator reads the correct answers. Respondents score their own assessments. *(Note to the facilitator:* Even answers to "objective" tests of cognitive knowledge are subject to some disagreement by academicians and diversity practitioners. The Diversity Awareness Assessment Scoring Key provides sources for the answers given; these sources represent the most accurate information currently available. But invariably some respondents will challenge even the "objective" data.)

---

[1] This instrument is excerpted from *Questions of Diversity,* edited by George F. Simons and Bob Abramms, which is available from Pfeiffer & Company.

It is suggested that the respondents form subgroups of two or three members each. With their partner(s), they may discuss questions such as the following:

- Question and answers that were surprising.
- Questions that were very easy.
- Answers that resulted in confusion or discomfort.

After, the facilitator may reconvene the total group and lead a closing discussion of the assessment and the subgroups' conclusions.

SUGGESTED USES

Following are some benefits from using this assessment:

- Helping those who believe they have no knowledge gaps or no need for additional learning.
- Demonstrating that every individual regardless of her/his diversity category has more to learn.
- Providing a vehicle for participants to ask additional diversity questions in a "safe" climate in which others are also acknowledging their information needs or knowledge gaps.
- Providing opportunities for participants to affirm to others and themselves how they also possess some diversity knowledge and expertise that can be shared with others.
- Verifying that participants from all "obvious" and "less obvious" diversity categories have varying levels of knowledge about diversity issues.

David P. Tulin is president and lead trainer of Tulin DiversiTeam Associates, an interracial/intergender team specializing in multicultural training, diversity team building, and sexual-harassment prevention/intervention programs. Their clients include corporations, universities, law firms, government agencies, community groups, law enforcement personnel, schools, unions, and hospitals. Mr. Tulin is the recipient of a number of awards in intergroup human-relations training, mediation, and management education. He is known for dealing with issues of sexual harassment, work force diversity, team building, and leadership development in a spirit that taps the synergy of diversity for greater productivity, managerial growth, and organizational improvement. He is also associated with ODT and works on a variety of multicultural projects, including Questions of Diversity, *a collection of assessment tools.*

DIVERSITY AWARENESS ASSESSMENT

David P. Tulin

Instructions: Circle the correct answer to the questions that follow. You are not expected to know all of the answers; for those answers you do not know, choose the answer that seems most likely to be correct.

1. Women who assume jobs that have been traditionally held by men often experience difficulty because

   a. they are not used to the work.

   b. their skills have to be upgraded.

   c. they are kept on the outside by male coworkers.

   d. they are distracted by the male dominated environment.

2. Provisions of the Americans with Disabilities Act prohibit an employer from inquiring into a job applicant's disability with questions concerning

   a. mental illness.

   b. age.

   c. past work experience.

   d. religious affiliation.

3. Today's preferred term, used in law and everyday life, is

   a. physically challenged.

   b. person with a disability.

   c. handicapped.

   d. crippled.

4. When a woman is in control of a communication dynamic with a man, she prefers to stand

   a. closer to the man than he would prefer to stand to her.

   b. farther from the man than he would prefer to stand from her.

   c. the same distance from the man that he would prefer to stand from her.

---

5. The "glass ceiling" theory in organizational life refers to

   a. the effect of indirect lighting on employee motivation.

   b. the high expectations, but frustrating limits, that women and minorities experience in promotions.

   c. the hiring of entry level and female employees with the clear opportunity for future promotions based on performance.

   d. the feeling that many minorities and women experience of being constantly watched and supervised by those above them.

6. One of the most common complaints of employees with physically handicapping conditions is

   a. they are constantly taken care of by coworkers.

   b. they are treated as though they are invisible.

   c. they are asked to perform duties beyond their capabilities.

   d. they are regularly asked about their physical conditions.

7. Women in blue-collar, male-dominated occupations are physically sexually harassed more often than their female white collar counterparts; they are

   a. less assertive in resisting and reporting it.

   b. more assertive in resisting and reporting it.

   c. equally assertive in resisting and reporting it.

   d. more assertive in resisting, but less likely to report it.

8. Of those taking advantage of parental leave, child care, and flex-time benefits,

   a. 90 percent are women and 10 percent are men.

   b. 60 percent are women and 40 percent are men.

   c. 75 percent are women and 25 percent are men.

   d. 50 percent are women and 50 percent are men.

9. Affirmative Action programs are designed to

   a. give preference to female and minority candidates who may be somewhat less qualified in order to make their numbers in the work force equal to white males.

   b. open access to potential employees who have previously been excluded from equal competition for jobs within particular organizations.

   c. fill a predetermined quota of women and minorities in an organization.

   d. have organizations look more affirmatively on women and minorities in job evaluations than they look on white males.

10. Based on 1993 research, sexual harassment costs the typical Fortune 500 company large sums of money each year as a result of low productivity, employee turnover, and absenteeism, with totals averaging in excess of

    a. $1 million yearly.

    b. $3 million yearly.

    c. $7 million yearly.

    d. $20 million yearly.

11. A person who says "Do you think Pat should be at this meeting?" clearly means something quite different from one who says "I think Pat should be at this meeting."

    a. True.

    b. False.

12. Efforts to integrate deaf people into conventional schools and to help them learn to speak English are causing fierce resistance from some activists within the deaf community because they

    a. consider deaf people simply as a linguistic minority who speak a different language.

    b. consider deaf people unteachable through conventional methods.

    c. consider it a waste of resources.

    d. wish to support deaf people by teaching them separately.

Pfeiffer & Company

13. Eighty-five percent of all human communication has no necessary relationship to the content of what is being said.

   a. True.

   b. False.

14. Placing persons with disabilities in a separate seating area at public events is often experienced by people with disabilities as

   a. the same as segregation.

   b. a reasonable accommodation.

   c. Neither a nor b.

   d. Both a and b.

15. According to the 1991 "Glass Ceiling" Report of the U.S. Department of Labor, women and minorities who were in higher management positions were almost always in

   a. line positions such as operations and production.

   b. line positions such as sales.

   c. staff positions such as human resources and public relations.

   d. temporary positions.

16. When employees have good communication skills, work teams have been shown to be more creative and productive when they are composed of people who

   a. come from the same area of professional specialization.

   b. have similar work and communication styles.

   c. come from similar cultural backgrounds.

   d. come from similar educational backgrounds.

   e. None of the above.

17. Among the costs that managers and their employers pay for "walking on egg shells" in supervising and communicating criticism and praise to female and minority employees is

    a. limiting the employee's ability to contribute to the organization.

    b. an increase in charges of discrimination.

    c. support for some white males who accuse the organization of unfair preferential treatment for minorities and women.

    d. increased probability that the female or minority employee will fail.

    e. All of the above.

18. Nonverbal cues in an interview that are good indicators of a candidate's high motivation are smiling, gesturing, good eye contact, and animated verbal interchange.

    a. True.

    b. False.

19. One of the most frequently cited factors that women and minorities have indicated as being helpful to their advancement to top executive levels in organizations has been

    a. the need to fill a minority quota.

    b. being seen as the best qualified candidate for the position.

    c. having the most experience.

    d. having been mentored and coached by significant organizational leaders.

20. An individual's claim of employment discrimination can be upheld if the use of a language that the employee does not understand has been used by a supervisor or colleague to prevent the employee from satisfactorily performing his or her job.

    a. True.

    b. False.

Diversity Awareness Assessment Scoring Key

1. C
2. A
3. B
4. B
5. B
6. B
7. A
8. B
9. B
10. C
11. B
12. A
13. A
14. D
15. C
16. E
17. E
18. B
19. D
20. A

Sources

1. "To Gentlemen Who Work with Ladies," *Philadelphia Inquirer,* May 16, 1993.

2. "The Disabilities Act Helps But," *The Wall Street Journal,* July 19, 1993.

3. "What's in a Label," *The Washington Post,* April 10, 1993.

4. Deborah Tannen, *You Just Don't Understand* (1990, New York: Morrow)

5. "A More Accurate Way to Measure Diversity," *Personnel Journal,* October 1993.

6. "The Disabilities Act Helps But," *The Wall Street Journal,* July 19, 1993.

7. "Sexual Harassment Issues: A Company Policy Concern," *South Florida Business Journal,* April 16, 1993 (because of fear of physical harm and social and supervisory retaliation).

8. "Leave Measure Imposes Broad Notion of Family," *The Wall Street Journal,* February 10, 1993.

9. "A More Accurate Way to Measure Diversity," *Personnel Journal,* October 1993.

10. "Harassment Costs All of Us Money," *US Woman Engineer,* May/June 1993.

11. Deborah Tannen, *You Just Don't Understand* (1990, New York: Morrow).

12. "Deafness As Culture," *The Atlantic Monthly,* September 1993.

13. Deborah Tannen, *You Just Don't Understand* (1990, New York: Morrow)

14. "Disabilities Act Brings Change to Show Floors," *Chicago Business*, April 12, 1993.

15. 1991 US Department of Labor Glass Ceiling Report.

16. "Managing Cultural Diversity: Implications for Organizational Competitiveness," *Academy of Management Executive,* 5(3).

17. "High Level Anxiety," *Working Woman Magazine,* 1992.

18. "A Measure of Success," Human Resource Executive Forum, 1992.

19. Survey results from Tulin DiversiTeam Associates participants, 1993.

20. "Only in America," *New York Law Journal,* October, 1993.

LIFE-ORIENTATION INVENTORY

Udai Pareek

Abstract: This inventory of life style is based on the
work of Bray, Campbell, and Grant (1974). In their
research, "enlarging style" was associated with more
career success, while "enfolding style" was associated
with less career success. Although predictors of career
success may change over time, knowing one's life-style
orientation and preferences can enhance understanding of individual differences.

The enlarging life style is oriented toward innovation, change, and growth. The enlarger looks for responsibility on the job and is likely also to seek and
achieve a position of influence in organizations. Self-
development activities are stressed.

The enfolding life style is oriented to the goals of
tradition, stability, and inner strength. Enfolders seek
to cultivate and solidify those things that invite attention within more familiar spheres. They like to settle
into tasks and see them through to a full conclusion.

This instrument uses an organizational and career
context to allow a person to assess his or her life-style
orientation within the framework of "enlarging" or
"enfolding."

Life-style orientation has been studied largely at the personal level. However, life style is rapidly becoming a consideration at the organizational level. People of "Generation X" do not respond to the same rewards and incentives as their predecessors did. Organizations increasingly face employees for whom life style is a major consideration in their decision making.

The concept of "life style" was originally proposed by Adler in 1930. Adler suggested three characteristics of "style of life": origin in the childhood, self-consistency, and constancy (Anabacher & Anabacher, 1956). Using the birth-order theory of Adler, Eckstein and Driscoll (1982) suggested ways of assessing life style in a group. Driscoll and Eckstein (1982) also proposed a fifty-item instrument to measure life styles and names of animals were used to represent five life styles: tigers (aggressive), chameleons (conforming), turtles (defensive), eagles (individualistic), and salmon (resistive). Adams (1980), in the context of stress, suggested a simple instrument that used three life-styles: personalistic, sociocentric, and formalistic. However, these instruments are not in the organizational and career contexts.

Various concepts have been proposed for life styles: core values and ideology (Bernard, 1975; Ginsberg, 1966), characteristic mode of living (Lazer, 1963), behavioral pattern with which the individual relates to external reality and internal dispositions (Zaleznik, 1977), pattern of preferences, values, and beliefs about oneself in regard to the work around the person (Friedlander, 1975).

Bray, Campbell, and Grant (1974), in an in-depth and longitudinal study of successful (fast upward movement) and less-successful executives in a well-known organization, identified a number of factors associated with career and role success and failure. Two distinct patterns emerged from groupings of these factors. The one associated with career success or job success was called "enlarging style," and the other (associated with less success) was called "enfolding style." The distinction between the two is contrasted below (based on Bray, Campbell, & Grant).

Enlarging Style

The enlarging life style is oriented toward the goal of innovation, change, and growth. The enlarger moves away from the tradition and places emphasis on adaptation, self-development, and the extension of influence outward, into the work and community spheres. The enlarger looks for responsibility on the job and is likely also to seek and achieve a position of influence in organizations. Self-development activities are stressed. Thus, enlargers are likely not only to read, attend the theater, and keep up with current events, but they might take courses and even respond to the promptings of physical fitness and health food.

At the same time, their earlier ties to parents and formal religious practices begin to weaken. Enlargers find that their values have changed so dramatically that they no longer enjoy the company of old friends in the neighborhoods of their childhood. Except for a certain nostalgia when visiting parents and relatives, they are not satisfied with the ties of yesterday. A complete commitment to one's religion is similarly less meaningful, particularly since the enlarger makes every effort to see alternative points of view and to lend himself or herself to new experiences of all varieties. This does not mean that enlargers always break off entirely from their religious groups, but some of them do.

Enfolding Style

The enfolding life style is oriented to the goals of tradition, stability, and inward strength. Rather than pitching their strength outward, enfolders seek to cultivate and solidify those things that invite attention within more familiar spheres. They are not joiners of social or community organizations, and when they do enter into these activities, they rarely seek active roles. They value parental ties and seek to keep a relationship active with childhood friends, if this is at all possible.

Enfolders may find it upsetting to leave their hometown areas, even if the move represents career advancement. In a new locale, they are likely to have considerable difficulty feeling at home. They are not likely to attend night college or to study on their own time unless they believe their efforts will directly bring job rewards. An enfolder may begin a self-improvement program, but his or her heart is seldom in it. He or she likes to settle into a job and see it through to a full conclusion, obtaining great satisfaction from a job well done.

The enfolder is not awed by fads. He or she forms a close attachment to a small circle of friends, and most of his or her socializing is done with relatives. Status consideration sometimes embarrasses enfolders, who value informality, sincerity, and genuineness in human affairs. Bray, Campbell, and Grant further describe an enfolder as follows:

> Peers and superiors have told him in the past that his attitude is not conducive to upward mobility on the job, but he had not been able to see their point at the time. It seemed to him that it was in the company's interest to keep their employees happy....

He has thought about leaving to enter his own business, but he lacks capital and has some doubts about whether the move would be worth the risk.... One could not consider this man to be unhappy, except in the sense that he somewhat feels embarrassed about his lack of advancement. (pp. 108-111)

THE INSTRUMENT

The Life-Orientation Inventory is based on the Bray, Campbell, and Grant (1974) description of enlargers and enfolders and also on case histories of the two styles. The Life-Orientation Inventory has two scales. Scale A contains fourteen activities pertaining to both orientations. The respondent indicates, on a five-point scale, the amount of time (compared to time spent by other people in his or her group) that he or she spends on each activity. Scale B consists of six pairs of forced-choice items. The respondent again indicates (on a five-point scale) the importance of the two activities when each is compared with the other.

Scoring

The Life-Orientation Inventory contains ten items pertaining to the enlarging style (A: 1, 3, 4, 7, 12, 13, 14; B: 2, 4, 6) and ten items pertaining to the enfolding style (A: 2, 5, 6, 8, 9, 10, 11; B: 1, 3, 5). Ratings on the ten items on the enlarging style are added, and the total score will range from 10 to 50. Ratings on the ten items on the enfolding style are added, and the total score will likewise range from 10 to 50. To convert the scores to percentage terms, use the following formula for each style: (total score - 10) x 2.5. Then the score for each style will range from 0 to 100. On the new scale, a score above 50 would indicate a tendency toward that style; and the higher the score, the higher the probability that the style fits the participant.

Reliability

Even-odd correlations of items—recalculated from Keshote's (1991) data—were .67 and .57, respectively, for enfolding and enlarging styles. The item total correlations ranged from .45 to .64 for enlarging and from .46 to .66 for enfolding scales. These are acceptable reliability figures.

Correlates of the Styles

Using data from about two hundred managers, Keshote (1991) reported correlation of 0.38 between the two styles (significant at .01 level). This is an unexpected finding and needs examination. There seem to be some common elements between the two styles. Correlation between the two for a smaller sample (twenty) was negative but not significant.

Keshote also reported a relationship between life-orientation styles and some personality variables: self-actualization, locus of control, interpersonal trust, power needs, and managerial styles. For self-actualization, the Inventory of Self-Actualization Characteristics (ISAC) by Banet (1976) was used. In ISAC, scores are obtained on sixteen aspects, and an overall score is also determined. Two aspects, number 3 (spontaneity, simplicity, and naturalness) and number 12 (ethical standards), were unrelated to either the enlarging or enfolding style. Correlations with six aspects (numbers 4, 5, 7, 9, 13, and 16) were significant for both the styles. These are shown in Table 1. Table 1 also gives correlations on aspects significant only for enfolders (numbers 8 and 10) and only for enlargers (numbers 1, 2, 6, 11, 14, 15).

Table 1. Significant Correlations Between Life-Orientation Inventory Styles and Self-Actualization Aspects

Self-Actualization Aspects	Enlargers	Enfolders
8. Capacity for peak experience		.30
10. Interpersonal relations		.19
1. Efficient reality perception	.25	
2. Acceptance of self, others, human nature	.16	
6. Autonomy of independence of culture and environment	.21	
11. Democratic character structure	.19	
14. Creativeness	.23	
15. Resistance of consultation	.22	
4. Problem-centeredness	.29	
7. Freshness of appreciation	.35	
5. Detachment and privacy	.18	.15
9. *Gemeinschaftsgefühl* (empathy for and helping others)	.22	.17
13. Unhostile sense of humor	.15	.23
16. Overall	.29	.21

The two items on which there is high correlation with enfolding style relate to existential orientation (both personal and interpersonal satisfaction). Regarding enlargers, all the items relate to autonomy (both of self and others). Therefore, whereas enlargers create autonomy, enfolders are people oriented. Enfolders have higher correlations with sense of humor, and enlargers have higher correlations with problem centeredness, freshness of appreciation, and *gemeinschaftsgefühl* (identifying with all human beings or a desire to be helpful to others). A detailed discussion on the significance of the self-actualization dimensions can be found in Banet (1976).

No correlation was found with interpersonal trust. Both enfolding and enlarging styles had significant correlations with internal locus of control (.14 and .21, respectively). The correlations with external (others) and external (chance) were significant (negative correlation) only with the enlarging style.

> *Whereas enlargers create autonomy, enfolders are people oriented.*

Locus of control was measured by an instrument prepared on Levenson's (1973) model. Enlargers have low externality (both for others and for chance). On an instrument on power (Pareek, 1994), enlargers valued persuasive power (r = .18, significant) and did not feel its deficiency (r = -.13, significant). No other correlation was significant.

Using the transactional analysis model of managerial styles, Pareek (1984) found that both enfolding and enlarging styles had positive correlation with operating effectiveness of the adult ego state (problem solving, .12 and .16, respectively), whereas the enfolding style had significant negative correlation with operating effectiveness of regulating parent. Enfolders seem to impose their norms on their subordinates, whereas both enlargers and enfolders have task effectiveness. No other correlations were significant.

In summary, although the two styles seem to have a few things in common, enfolders are more people oriented and less effective in developing self-managing norms. Enlargers are effective in creating autonomy and attribute results less to others and chance. Enlargers seem to be more effective executives.

Administration and Uses of the Inventory

The Life-Orientation Inventory can be used for both research and human resource development (HRD). Although instructions are provided on the inventory, a facilitator should be available to clarify the instructions. The participants can score their own inventories. If they are concerned about some of the elements, they may discuss them in small groups of their choice and plan ways to alter the profiles.

146

References

Adams, T.D. (1980). *Understanding and managing stress: A workbook in changing life styles.* San Diego, CA: Pfeiffer & Company.

Anabacher, H.Z., & Anabacher, R. (Eds.). (1956). *The individual psychology of Alfred Adler.* London: George Allen & Irwin.

Banet, A.G. (1976). Inventory of self-actualization characteristics (ISAC). In J.W. Pfeiffer & J.E. Jones (Eds.), *The 1976 annual for facilitators, trainers, and consultants* (pp. 67-77). San Diego, CA: Pfeiffer & Company.

Bernard, J. (1975). Notes on changing life styles. *Journal of Marriage and Family, 53,* 582-593.

Bray, D.W., Campbell, R.J., & Grant, D.L. (1974). *Formative years in business: A long-term AT&T study of managerial lives.* New York: John Wiley.

Driscoll, R., & Eckstein, D.G. (1982). Life style questionnaire. In J.W. Pfeiffer & L.D. Goodstein (Eds.), *The 1982 annual for facilitators, trainers, and consultants* (pp. 100-107). San Diego, CA: Pfeiffer & Company.

Eckstein, D.G., & Driscoll, R. (1982). An introduction to lifestyle assessment. In J.W. Pfeiffer & L.D. Goodstein (Eds.), *The 1982 annual for facilitators, trainers, and consultants* (pp. 182-189). San Diego, CA: Pfeiffer & Company.

Friedlander, F. (1975). Emergent and contemporary life styles: An inter-generational issue. *Human Relations, 28,* 329-341.

Ginsberg, E. (1966). *Life styles of educated women.* New York: Columbia University Press.

Keshote, K.K. (1991). *Correlates of conflict management.* Unpublished doctoral dissertation, Gujarat University, Gujarat, India.

Lazer, W. (1963). Life style concept and marketing. In S. Greyser (Ed.), *Towards scientific marketing* (pp. 140-151). New York: AMA.

Levenson, H. (1973). Multidimensional locus of control in psychiatric patients. *Journal of Consulting and Clinical Psychology, 41,* 387-404.

Pareek, U. (1984). Interpersonal styles: SPIRO-M. In J.W. Pfeiffer & L.D. Goodstein (Eds.), *The 1984 annual for facilitators, trainers, and consultants* (pp. 119-130). San Diego, CA: Pfeiffer & Company.

Pareek, U. (1994). *Coercive and persuasive power scale.* Unpublished manuscript.

Zaleznik, A. (1977). Leaders and managers: Are they different? *Harvard Business Review, 55,* 67-78.

Udai Pareek, Ph.D., is Chairman of the Institute of Development Studies, Jaipur; the Jaipur HRD Research Foundation; and the Scientific Advisory Committee of the Indian Institute of Health Management Research. He has been president of the National HRD Network and the Indian Society of Applied Behavioural Sciences. Dr. Pareek is an adjunct professor of health policy and administration at the University of North Carolina at Chapel Hill. He has served as USAID OD advisor to the Ministry of Health of the Government of Indonesia and director of the School of Basic Sciences and Humanities (and Dean of Social Sciences) at the University of Udaipur. Dr. Pareek consults with a large number of Indian and international organizations.

LIFE-ORIENTATION INVENTORY

Udai Pareek

Name _____

Organization _____

Date _____

Instructions for Part A: The purpose of the Life-Orientation Inventory (Bray, Campbell, & Grant, 1974) is to obtain profiles of managers' life orientations. There are no right or wrong answers. For Part A, ask yourself how much time and energy you spend on each activity listed. Then decide how that time and energy compares with the time and energy other members of your group (profession, occupation, level of employment, etc.) are probably spending on that activity. Although you cannot know exactly how much time and energy others spend, your perception is what is important in this inventory. Therefore, circle the number that seems to apply to you, as follows:

Circle 1 if: You spend much less time and energy than the average for your group (i.e., your amounts of time and energy are among the lowest 5 percent).

Circle 2 if: You spend somewhat less time and energy than the average for your group (i.e., your amounts are higher than the lowest 5 percent but still among the lowest 20 percent).

Circle 3 if: You spend about the same amount of time and energy as the average for your group (i.e., your amounts are in the middle 60 percent).

Circle 4 if: You spend somewhat more time and energy than the average for your group (i.e., your amounts are among the highest 20 percent but still lower than the top 5 percent).

Circle 5 if: You spend much more time and energy than the average for your group (i.e., your amounts are among the highest 5 percent).

The 1995 Annual: Volume 1, Training.
Copyright © 1995 by Pfeiffer & Company, San Diego, CA.

	Lowest 5%	Low 5%-20%	Middle 60%	High 5%-20%	Highest 5%
1. Reading to broaden knowledge.	1	2	3	4	5
2. Being with your spouse and children.	1	2	3	4	5
3. Exercising to improve physical fitness (swimming, jogging, etc.).	1	2	3	4	5
4. Attending courses for self-development.	1	2	3	4	5
5. Engaging in religious activities.	1	2	3	4	5
6. Engaging in spiritual pursuits or activities.	1	2	3	4	5
7. Acquiring financial assets (shares, real estate, etc.).	1	2	3	4	5
8. Dealing with problems/matters of your family members.	1	2	3	4	5
9. Contacting and meeting with friends and associates.	1	2	3	4	5
10. Engaging in leisure-oriented activities (hobbies, sports, etc.).	1	2	3	4	5
11. Socializing (at parties or clubs, with small groups, etc.).	1	2	3	4	5
12. Taking part in professional associations, societies, activities.	1	2	3	4	5
13. Contributing to community service.	1	2	3	4	5

	Lowest 5%	Low 5%-20%	Middle 60%	High 5%-20%	Highest 5%
14. Finding and implementing new ways to increase efficiency, commitment of employees, etc.	1	2	3	4	5

Instructions for Part B: Part B presents six pairs of items. Look at each pair and decide which of the two is more important to you. Circle the number that applies to you, as follows:

Circle 1 if: "a" is clearly more important to you than "b" is.
Circle 2 if: "a" is somewhat more important to you than "b" is.
Circle 3 if: "a" and "b" are equally important to you.
Circle 4 if: "b" is somewhat more important to you than "a" is.
Circle 5 if: "b" is clearly more important to you than "a" is.

	"a" Clearly More Important	"a" Somewhat More Important	Both Equally Important	"b" Somewhat More Important	"b" Clearly More Important
1a. Work demands.					
1b. Demands made by family members.	1	2	3	4	5
2a. Concern for job content.					
2b. Concern for job benefits and other advantages.	1	2	3	4	5
3a. Concern for your own family.					
3b. Concern for rapid promotions.	1	2	3	4	5
4a. Job placement in your home town or other desired place.					
4b. A challenging and interesting job.	1	2	3	4	5
5a. Taking responsibility in a professional/community-service organization.					
5b. Spending time with parents, relatives, or friends.	1	2	3	4	5

Pfeiffer & Company

	"a" Clearly More Important	"a" Somewhat More Important	Both Equally Important	"b" Somewhat More Important	"b" Clearly More Important
6a. Continuing and concentrating on a job for a long time.					
6b. Searching for and obtaining a job that will give better career Opportunities in the future.	1	2	3	4	5

Reference

Bray, D.W., Campbell, R.J., & Grant, D.L. (1974). *Formative years in business: A long-term AT&T study of managerial lives*. New York: John Wiley.

Life-Orientation Inventory Scoring and Interpretation Sheet

Instructions: Transfer the value of the numbers that you circled on the Life-Orientation Inventory to the blanks below. To determine your percentage score, total each column. Subtract ten from each total, then multiply by 2.5. Scores above 50% for either style indicate a tendency toward that style; the higher the percentage, the greater the probability that that style fits you.

Enlarging Style	Enfolding Style
A1 _____	A2 _____
A3 _____	A5 _____
A4 _____	A6 _____
A7 _____	A8 _____
A12 _____	A9 _____
A13 _____	A10 _____
A14 _____	A11 _____
B2 _____	B1 _____
B4 _____	B3 _____
B6 _____	B5 _____
Total_____	**Total**_____

Total Enlarging Score _____ - 10 = _____ x 2.5 = _____%

Total Enfolding Score _____ - 10 = _____ x 2.5 = _____%

The 1995 Annual: Volume 1, Training.
Copyright © 1995 by Pfeiffer & Company, San Diego, CA.

Introduction
to the Presentation and Discussion Resources Section

Learning based on direct experience is not the only kind of learning appropriate to human-interaction training. A practical combination of theory and research with experiential learning generally enriches training and may be essential in many types of cognitive and skill development. Affective and cognitive data support, alter, validate, extend, and complement each other. Each facilitator needs to develop a repertoire of theory and background that he or she can use in a variety of situations.

The 1995 Annual: Volume 1, Training includes thirteen articles, in the following categories:

Individual Development: Life/Career Planning

The Flexible Career: Riding the Career Waves of the Nineties, by Caela Farren (page 207)

Problem Solving: Conflict

Managing Conflict and Disagreement Constructively, by Herbert S. Kindler (page 169)

Problem Solving: Change and Change Agents

The Changing Organization: New Challenges for HRD Professionals and Managers, by Robert William Lucas (page 191)

Applying Business Process Improvement to a Training Department, by Beverly Ann Scott (page 261)

Understanding Change from the Gestalt Perspective, by Hank Karp (page 271)

Groups and Teams: Types of Groups
General Inclusion Groups Versus Individual Initiative Networks, by Stanley M. Herman (page 199)

Groups and Teams: Behavior and Roles in Groups
Creating and Motivating Effective Teams: The Challenge, by William A. Snow (page 251)

Facilitating: Techniques and Strategies
Using Experiential Learning to Improve Quality, by Ellie S. Browner and Robert C. Preziosi (page 175)

Sensitive-Subject Training: Considerations for Trainers, by Daphne DePorres (page 243)

Leadership: Strategies and Techniques
Delivering Feedback: The First Step, Not the Last, by John Geirland and Marci Maniker-Leiter (page 155)

Leadership Styles and the Enneagram, by Patrick J. Aspell and Dee Dee Aspell (page 227)

Leadership: Top-Management Issues and Concerns
Motivation in Work Settings Today: A Reductionist Approach, by Thomas H. Patten, Jr. (page 215)

Doing More with Less: How to Increase Productivity, by Stephen R. Grossman (page 279)

As with every *Annual,* this volume covers a variety of topics; not every article will appeal to every reader. Nevertheless, the range of articles presented should encourage a good deal of thought-provoking, serious discussion about the present and the future of HRD. Other articles on specific subjects can be located by using the "Experiential Learning Activities Categories" chart that follows, or by using our comprehensive *Reference Guide to Handbooks and Annuals.* This book, which is updated regularly, indexes all of the *Annuals* and all of the *Handbooks of Structured Experiences* that we have published to date. With each revision, the *Reference Guide* becomes a complete, up-to-date, and easy-to-use resource for selecting appropriate materials from *all* of the *Annuals* and *Handbooks.*

DELIVERING FEEDBACK:
THE FIRST STEP, NOT THE LAST

John Geirland and Marci Maniker-Leiter

Abstract: Trainers and consultants are continually called on to provide feedback to clients. Feedback takes a variety of forms: individual feedback in the classroom, group feedback in the classroom, 360-degree leader feedback, organization-wide survey feedback, and unit survey feedback.

In this article, the authors contrast the classic feedback model with an iterative model for delivering feedback. They outline facilitation techniques to use with feedback and explore common emotional responses to feedback. Finally, the authors touch on common concerns and dilemmas that change agents face when they deliver feedback, including ethical considerations, confidentiality, and maintaining the self-esteem of participants.

Although they differ in the type of courses, tools, and techniques they employ, nearly all trainers and consultants have one thing in common: They provide feedback to clients. The ability to provide relatively objective feedback—whether it pertains to social style, organizational climate, or leadership skills—is one of the primary assets of change agents.[1] Although clients often pay significant fees to obtain this feedback, they often respond in the following ways:

- Silence.
- "It's good feedback, thanks"—followed by inaction.
- Superficial acceptance, leaving the change agent with a nagging feeling that the group did not understand.
- Anger, with a refusal to come to terms with the feedback.

These all-too-typical responses may be accounted for, in large part, by client resistance. However, matters are not helped by a common belief that the job of change agents is finished once they deliver the feedback. Feedback is not a one-time activity, a kind of data dump, but an iterative process, wherein the first cycle of feedback stimulates the client, or client organization, to bring forth more data and insights, which can be reanalyzed and cycled through again.

Approaching feedback as an iterative process enables the change agent to help the client realize deeper insights, ultimately reaching the most meaningful issues. This article describes a model for delivering feedback, outlines facilitation techniques, explores common emotional responses, and touches on common concerns and dilemmas that change agents face when they deliver feedback. Before embarking on a discussion of the model, this article outlines forms of feedback.

FORMS OF FEEDBACK

Feedback is usually delivered by change agents in two contexts: (a) the classroom and (b) as part of a consulting assignment. In both situations, feedback may be presented to individuals or groups that vary in size from several people to entire organizations. Specific forms of feedback include

---

[1] Because this article addresses both trainers and internal and external consultants, the more general term "change agent" is used to signify these groups.

individual feedback in the classroom, group feedback in the classroom, 360-degree leader feedback, organization-wide survey feedback, and unit survey feedback.

Individual Feedback (Classroom)

Many courses are designed around an individual assessment tool or use such a tool as an integral part of the course. An example is a social-style or management-style inventory. Typically, inventories are completed by participants prior to the class and may also be collected from the participant's associates. Inventory results are usually presented to participants during the course. This feedback often remains confidential, although participants can share the results with others if they choose.

Group Feedback (Classroom)

Formal group feedback in the classroom is less common, though a trainer may offer informal feedback to a class on a variety of process issues (e.g., "Our energy level seems low."). Formal group feedback is more appropriate when a natural work team participates in a class. Feedback for a team often focuses on team dynamics, such as quality of communication, cooperation, and sense of shared goals.

360-Degree Leader Feedback

A change agent may be brought in to assess a manager's or executive's leadership style. Interviews are conducted with the subject and the people who report to him or her, colleagues, and the subject's manager—a full circle of interviews, hence the name. Interviews may be augmented by the use of an instrument or inventory. Feedback is delivered confidentially, although the subject's manager may also hear the feedback.

Survey Feedback (Organization-Wide)

This category includes climate surveys and other organization-wide surveys in which the total population (or a random sample drawn from the population) completes a questionnaire assessing various aspects of organizational life and performance (e.g., job satisfaction, teamwork, goals, managing change, and communication). Quantitative responses are tabulated and open-ended (i.e., written) comments are content analyzed. If data are collected in interviews or focus groups, this information is also included. Feedback is delivered in the form of a report and/or presentation to management. Additional presentations may be made to staff, or a summary memo may be circulated. Individuals' survey responses remain confidential.

Survey Feedback (Unit)

Often as part of an organization-wide survey, feedback will be presented to individual work units, departments, or job classifications or levels. These results are often compared to the organization-wide base to provide a bench mark for the group in question. Usually the findings for one unit are not shared with people in other units.

THE MODEL

Before describing the iterative feedback model, this article reviews the classic feedback model, the one on which much training and organization work is implicitly based.

The Classic Feedback Model

The classic feedback model is often portrayed as a circular process, as shown in Figure 1.

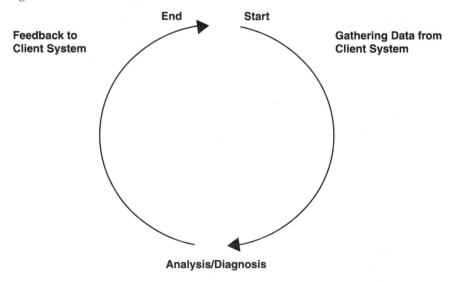

Figure 1. The Classic Feedback Model

Data are gathered from the client system by the change agent through one or more of the following methods:

- Interviews
- Focus groups
- Surveys
- Inventories (e.g., social-style inventory)
- Classroom activities
- Archival research (e.g., review of internal documents, such as financial, marketing, and customer-service reports)

These data are then analyzed by the change agent, sometimes in collaboration with the client, resulting in a set of observations, key issues, conclusions, recommendations, or diagnoses. This analysis, in principle, enables the client system to make adjustments in perceptions, behaviors, policies, and capabilities for enhancing individual or organizational performance. Often the change agent will then move into the next stage of consulting by working with the client to develop interventions for achieving needed changes. This classic model has been a useful guide to change agents for many years and has the added virtue of simplicity. However, the model does not capture the ways clients accept feedback.

The Iterative Feedback Model

In contrast to the one-cycle aspect of the classic model, the iterative feedback model (see Figure 2) presents the steps of gathering data, analysis, and feedback as an iterative process that involves at least two cycles. Furthermore, this model recognizes the complex emotional and cognitive responses that feedback can provoke.

Similar to the classic model, the iterative feedback model indicates that the change agent collects data from the client system, analyzes what he or she has collected, and feeds the information back to the client. Then some period of time follows in which the client processes the feedback. The client's emotional or cognitive responses following feedback will vary, depending on the nature of the feedback and the dynamics of the client system, but most will enter a "refractory period," where the process will, at least temporarily, stall. An analogy is the time a person takes to chew food before swallowing—the mastication period. This refractory period can last a few minutes or a few months—or even become a permanent block to further action.

Once the client has fully processed the initial feedback, the information can trigger additional observations, discussion, or insights by the client. These new data are again analyzed—often by mutual work by the client and

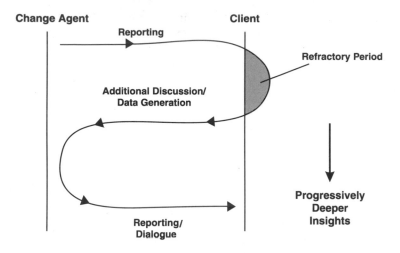

Figure 2. The Iterative Feedback Model

the change agent, creating more feedback for the client. On reflection, the client achieves deeper insights from the feedback, coming closer to the most important issues facing the client system. A second refractory period may follow, but this one is typically shorter and less pronounced than the first. The process may end here, or it may continue with additional iterations, particularly if new individuals or groups are brought in.

The following analogy may help clarify the model:

A man goes to his family doctor for a routine physical examination. The doctor takes the patient's vital signs, obtains urine and blood samples, and asks a few questions. Making an appointment for a return visit, the patient leaves.

Tests are performed on the blood and urine. When the patient returns, the physician shares the results of the tests: The patient has an elevated cholesterol count. The patient expresses disbelief. "But I watch what I eat! I eat hardly any red meat." The patient asks if the test is accurate. "Maybe someone's made a mistake." The physician tries to assure the patient that the test procedures are highly reliable.

The physician then asks the patient to keep a food journal (writing down everything he eats) the next week and also to bring in a family medical history, with cholesterol counts if possible. After much protest, the patient agrees.

At a subsequent appointment, the doctor and patient review the journal and the medical records. The patient's food journal shows that although he does not eat red meat, he consumes a lot of saturated fats from other sources. The patient's family has a history of heart disease and of elevated cholesterol.

After reviewing these items with his doctor, the patient accepts the diagnosis of high cholesterol and realizes it is an issue with which he must deal. He and the physician discuss other aspects of his health and life style, then develop a broad strategy for reducing the patient's cholesterol level.

This analogy illustrates the major aspects of the iterative feedback model, i.e., the initial period of data collection, the refractory period in which the patient's cognitive and emotional responses (disbelief, confusion) create resistance, working through the refractory period, additional data collection, and a collaborative effort to develop an intervention. Had the physician stopped with the initial report of results in the second visit, it is doubtful that the patient would have changed any of his habits that contributed to high cholesterol.

COMMON EMOTIONAL AND COGNITIVE RESPONSES TO FEEDBACK

For most people, receiving feedback is more than just an intellectual exercise; it is also an emotional experience. The type of feedback discussed here touches on aspects of work performance, management style, social style, how people relate to others (either as individuals or as part of a group), and other aspects of organizations. Usually these are issues that are of moderate to high concern and interest. Therefore, the occasion for feedback—often formally scheduled—brings with it a sense of drama, anticipation, and sometimes fear. The emotional and cognitive responses that feedback engenders will vary in intensity from person to person and situation to situation. Still, these responses often involve the five stages that Elisabeth Kubler-Ross (1969) described for people confronting death and dying:

- Shock and denial
- Anger
- Bargaining
- Depression
- Acceptance

Shock and Denial

The client receives feedback that is at variance to his or her beliefs, assumptions, or expectations. The feedback is often greeted with silence. The client may feel overwhelmed or confused at this point. Even if the information does not challenge important beliefs, assumptions, or expectations, the volume of feedback—particularly with surveys—may be temporarily paralyzing.

The lead author of this article once provided an executive with highly negative feedback on her management performance. This true illustration provides an excellent example of all five stages. During most of the initial feedback session, the manager listened passively and made few remarks. Her blank expression during the presentation showed no emotion. Even after the presentation, she could do little more than nod and acknowledge that she understood but disagreed with the findings.

Anger

If the feedback is negative or challenges deeply held beliefs, the client may feel threatened and react with anger. Continuing the example above, the executive later phoned the author to complain about the feedback she had received. "I'm a little teed off about it," she said. "In fact, I'm kind of angry at you."

The client now marshals his or her defenses, challenging the consultant's methods, the quality or completeness of the information, or the truthfulness of the people who provided the data. During the phone call described above, the client proceeded to challenge the methods used ("You based everything on one person's opinions."[2]) and the motives of participants ("They resent having to work so hard, so they're using the survey to get back at management.").

Bargaining

The client may begin to accept the truthfulness of the findings but seek to find explanations that prevent having to change behavior, beliefs, or assumptions. The executive in the example, in a later meeting, explained that her staff's responses were probably influenced by one of several events that had occurred at the time of the survey ("That was a very busy period for us, and they were probably burned out.").

Depression

Once the client realizes that change is necessary and inevitable, he or she may experience a sense of loss; depending on the nature of the feedback, he

---

[2] The feedback was, in fact, based on interviews with sixteen individuals and survey data from forty-four employees.

or she may even enter a period of depression. In many cases, the client is confronted with the loss of a cherished but inaccurate self-image. In our example, the executive began to make statements such as "This makes me want to just give up and retire," and "After all those years of hard work! If this gets out, my reputation will be ruined." The reality was that the client's reputation had already been questioned as a result of serious performance issues in her organization.

Acceptance

The client finally works through his or her resistance to the feedback. This acceptance signals the end of the refractory period in the iterative feedback model. The client has begun to make adjustments in his or her belief system to accommodate the new information. The change in beliefs and assumptions enables the client to offer new observations, perceptions, and insights, thus beginning the next cycle of data gathering, analysis, and feedback.

The executive in the example eventually accepted the indication that major changes were needed in the way she managed her organization. She began to explore key issues in greater depth and to plan future interventions to make changes.

HELPFUL FACILITATION SKILLS

The iterative feedback model requires a high degree of interaction with the client. Facilitation skills are essential to the process, and the change agent should be adept at the following:

- Active listening;
- The use of probes;
- Summarizing what people are saying;
- Clarifying comments;
- Keeping the individual or group on target and within time frames;
- Defusing emotional reactions;
- Creating conditions that encourage open and free dialogue; and
- Dealing with nonconstructive or disruptive behavior.

Additionally, the change agent must be sensitive to the type of emotional and cognitive responses that clients provide when first receiving feedback, as described above. He or she must read those responses correctly and not overreact in return.

Finally, the change agent must have the ability to help clients to integrate the new information they are bringing out in response to the feedback. Often this requires the change agent to help the client reframe the information that was previously collected (i.e., challenging basic assumptions, seeing the connections between issues, and, if necessary, changing the focus of the discussion).

STRATEGIES FOR DELIVERING FEEDBACK

A discussion of feedback strategies could easily fill a book and is well beyond the scope of this article. Nevertheless, we offer a few techniques that have worked well for us and others.

Individual Feedback (Classroom)

When individual feedback is provided in a classroom situation, an opportunity for participants to work through their emotional and cognitive responses can be provided by dividing the group into coaching pairs. One person in each pair asks the other person a series of clarifying and exploratory questions regarding the feedback he or she received. These questions might include the following:

- What are the surprises in this feedback? Why are you surprised?
- What part of this feedback are you comfortable with and what part makes you uncomfortable? Why?
- Provide me with an example that illustrates [an issue identified in the feedback].
- What other thoughts or ideas does this feedback trigger?

Once the recipient and his or her partner have worked through the questions, the pair switches roles and repeats the activity. This approach also provides the individual with an opportunity to generate more information and reach a deeper understanding of the issues.

360-Degree Leader Feedback

A 360-degree feedback session usually involves a one-on-one exchange between the client and the change agent. However, subsequent sessions can be enriched if the client agrees to allow his or her manager or associates to attend and offer reactions to the feedback (Does it sound accurate? Is it relevant? Any surprises?). The client and manager can then work together to design an action plan based on work assignments and opportunities. This approach requires a high degree of trust on the part of all parties. Nonetheless, the payback for all concerned can be substantial.

Group Feedback (Classroom or Survey)

One effective approach for delivering survey feedback is to present the data to successive (and representative) groups of employees from the target organization. Survey findings are presented in the form of summary bullets and bar charts. The results are delivered in one pass-through, which is followed by a question-and-answer period, then a break. Following the break, participants are divided into smaller groups (typically of two to five people). The groups are asked to review the survey findings and to do the following:

- Identify the three most important issues;
- Describe the conditions or factors that cause or influence the issues; and
- Write out questions that these issues raise.

The groups come together and share what they have developed. The new information is discussed, and the session ends with a greater understanding of the key issues identified in the survey. A set of questions is developed for further inquiry, and a follow-up session is then scheduled.

Classroom feedback can also follow this general procedure.

Customer-Service Model

Feedback repetition is even more effective when a group is receiving feedback about itself. One elegant variation is an adaptation from Chip Bell's (1994) technique for collecting customer-service feedback. In the customer-service model, customers sit around a table and describe their experiences related to customer service. Surrounding the table is an inner circle of first-line customer-service providers, who speak only when necessary to clarify or explain something to the customers. Surrounding the customer-service providers is an outer circle of managers. The managers are to listen only.

Immediately following the first round of feedback, the customers leave. The customer-service providers move to the table, and the managers move to the inner circle of chairs. The process begins again with customer-service providers giving feedback on the support and direction they receive from management.

This process could be adapted to any operational arena. Essentially, the organizational chart is inverted and the employees become the ultimate customers of management. In this scenario, first-line employees are at the table, supervisors sit in the inner circle of chairs, and managers are seated in the outer circle of chairs. Eventually, the first-line employees leave, and the others move inward. This approach allows for successive iterations of feedback, one wave building upon the next.

Common Concerns and Dilemmas

Delivering feedback is never simple. The circumstances in which the feedback is offered presents the change agent and client with a range of thorny issues—ethical considerations, confidentiality concerns, the self-esteem of participants—all balanced by the needs of the organization. Following are observations on each of these issues.

Ethical Considerations. "Knowledge is power," as the saying goes. The kind of information that is collected in individual and organizational assessments is very powerful. The goal of the change agent is to enable the client to use this information constructively and wisely for personal and organizational growth. On the other hand, feedback also has the potential to be damaging. For this reason, some organizations fear losing control of climate-survey data and will restrict access to it—though doing so often ends up being self-defeating. The change agent's primary ethical obligation is to ensure that individual and organizational assessments are carefully analyzed, appropriately interpreted, and presented in the proper context.

> *Delivering feedback is never simple.*

Confidentiality. More often than not, interviews, focus groups, and surveys are conducted under the rule of confidentiality, i.e., the provision that responses of individuals will not be revealed. Confidentiality is important and necessary to ensure that the responses being provided are candid and truthful. Sometimes the change agent will learn things that can have important consequences for an individual or organization but will be unable to share this information because doing so would violate the confidentiality rule.

The change agent may wonder what to do in these circumstances. Sometimes he or she can generalize the information enough to convey the point without betraying the respondent. In general, unless the matter involves life or death, change agents must respect the confidentiality of the people who share information with them. Nothing justifies breaching the confidentiality rule and dealing with the inevitable loss of trust that would follow.

Maintaining Self-Esteem. Feedback can be wounding to the self-esteem of individuals, groups, and even organizations. The question, "What does the change agent do if the news is bad?" frequently arises. As much as possible, he or she should present the feedback in a balanced fashion, beginning with positive items before moving on to the negative ones. The change agent should also focus on the issue or behavior rather than making judgments about the intrinsic qualities of individuals or organizations.

The client's self-esteem is more likely to be preserved if one says, "Your colleagues feel you could be more accessible during the day," instead of "Your colleagues think you're anti-social." However, the change agent should never avoid giving bad news; doing so is a disservice to the client.

CONCLUSION

An old consulting maxim states, "The presenting problem is not the problem." Often what appears to be a key problem or issue—the event or condition that prompted the client to bring in the change agent—is only a symptom. The feedback model presented in this paper, with its emphasis on client participation and an iterative approach to data collection and analysis, will enable change agents and clients to address the most meaningful issues facing them.

References

Bell, C. (1994, July 19). Customer retention: The power of customers as partners. Paper presented at the Institute of Management Studies, Los Angeles, CA.

Kubler-Ross, E. (1969). *On death and dying.* New York: Macmillan.

John G. Geirland, Ph.D., heads up Geirland & Associates, an organization management consulting firm based in Studio City, California, specializing in individual and organizational assessment, team development, managing change, and organizational design. Dr. Geirland has consulted to a wide range of public and private organizations, including the Department of Transportation, Blue Cross Blue Shield of Florida, General Dynamics, Great Western Bank, and the Los Angeles County Department of Mental Health, among others. He has published papers on organizational design, the impact of technology in organizations, leadership and values, and creativity.

__Marci Maniker-Leiter__ is a management and organizational development consultant with over fifteen years of experience in the financial services industry. Her clients include the University of California at Los Angeles, Home Savings of America, Salomon Brothers, Manufacturers Hanover Bank, and Strategic Consulting, Inc. As an internal consultant, she established and managed the organization development department at Great Western Bank. Ms. Maniker-Leiter received her master's degree in organizational psychology from Columbia University.

MANAGING CONFLICT AND DISAGREEMENT CONSTRUCTIVELY

Herbert S. Kindler

Abstract: A vital part of a trainer's or consultant's repertoire is being able to manage—and teach others to manage—conflict and disagreements. The five-mode model, for managing conflict, introduced in 1964 by Blake and Mouton, was useful in stable organizational environments. However, today's rapid changes in organizational systems and technologies require more skills and more options.

This article introduces three core principles to apply when engaging in conflict management, nine strategies—with varying degrees of flexibility and intensity—that can be selected or combined when dealing with others in a conflict situation, and a systematic process for diagnosing, planning, implementing, and following up any attempt to manage conflict and disagreement constructively.

It is common to hear people in organizations say something like the following about disagreement:

- "I hate the endless arguing—and feeling trapped by having to listen to someone's stored-up anger."
- "Nothing is less productive than dancing around our differences. People don't really change their minds."

Unskillfully or insensitively managed conflict results in bickering, bruised feelings, wasted time, and unproductive rivalry. In contrast, when disagreement is handled well, opportunities arise for learning, cooperative work, and creative ideas. Teamwork improves, stress is reduced, trust is built, and people feel more committed to agreed-on decisions.

THE CONCEPTS

Managing conflict well requires conceptual tools, sensitivity, and practice. To facilitate the constructive resolution of conflict, a five-mode model (Blake and Mouton, 1964) was introduced. This model is still used by many consultants because it is easy to teach and learn. It was adequate when technology and the competitive environment were more stable. Nevertheless, contemporary managers need all the help they can get to improve productivity and maintain staff commitment. A research-based, comprehensive, nine-strategies model for managing conflict and disagreement (Kindler, 1994) is better suited for use in flatter organizations that experience more fluid relationships.

The following sections contain three core principles, nine strategies, and a four-step process (Figure 1) that can help any consultant's success rate in dealing with conflict.

Principles for Managing Conflict and Disagreement Constructively

1. *Maintain mutual respect.* Ask yourself, "How can I discuss our differences in ways that allow the other person to retain his or her dignity? How can I avoid having the other person feel denigrated or 'put down'?"

2. *Seek common ground.* Explore your overarching goals, values, and shared purpose. Try to see things through the other person's eyes

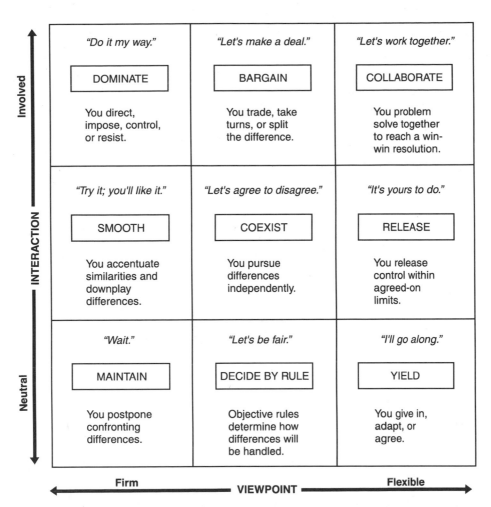

Figure 1. Nine Strategies for Managing Conflict and Disagreement Constructively[1]

    (e.g., his or her culture, race, gender, age, or life experiences). Don't lock yourself into adversarial or polarized positions.

3. Deal with disagreement after choosing an appropriate level of *flexibility and involvement.* The more you can learn from the other person, the more you can gain from a flexible stance. The more a good working relationship is desired, the more personal should be your interaction.

Strategies for Managing Conflict and Disagreement Constructively

Conflict and disagreement can be handled most effectively by employing a wide range of approaches. In a research study to understand actual behavior (Kindler, 1983), people were asked the following: "When your views on a work-related issue differ from the views of others who are also importantly involved, how do you prepare for such situations?" From the responses, two behaviors emerged as themes:

- Deciding how firm or flexible to be when asserting one's viewpoint, and

- Choosing how intensely involved to be with others who hold divergent views.

After these two dimensions—viewpoint flexibility and interaction intensity—were identified, a study of the literature on conflict revealed the following nine strategies, which are depicted in Figure 1.

Dominate. Using power and pressure when speed or confidentiality are important or when the situation is too minor to warrant time-consuming involvement of others. Also for self-protection against people who would use their power abusively.

Smooth. Gaining acceptance of one's views by accentuating the benefits and smoothing over disadvantages that would fuel opposition.

Maintain. Holding onto the status quo by deferring action on views that differ from one's own. Useful as an interim strategy when time is needed to collect information or to let emotions cool down.

Bargain. Offering something the other party wants in exchange for something one wants. Expedient when time pressures preclude collaboration. A mediator may facilitate this strategy.

Coexist. Determining jointly to follow separate paths for an agreed-on period of time. Use when both parties are firm, and pilot testing will determine which path has greater merit.

Decide by Rule. Agreeing jointly to use an objective rule such as a vote, lottery, seniority system, or arbitration. Helpful when one wants to be seen as impartial but decisive action is needed.

Collaborate. Joint exploration to develop a creative solution that satisfies the important concerns of all parties. Useful when the issues are too important to be compromised, or when commitment is vital to successful implementation of the solution.

Release. Let go when the issue doesn't warrant your time or energy, or when you want others to resolve a non-critical issue to foster their initiative and provide a learning opportunity.

Yield. Support the other person's views when you become convinced it is more appropriate, or when the issue is much more important to them than to you.

It is a good idea to avoid overusing one or two habitual approaches. Rather, one should consciously choose the strategy—or blend of strategies—appropriate to the situation.

Process for Managing Conflict and Disagreement Constructively

As important as guiding principles are, and as helpful as a repertoire of strategies can be, a systematic process for dealing with conflict and disagreement is vital to producing desirable outcomes. The process consists of the following four steps:

Diagnosis. Monitoring where differences simmer in order to be able to handle the situation before it boils over into overt conflict. Potential sources of conflict are:

- Information is interpreted differently.
- Goals appear to be incompatible.
- Boundaries are violated.
- Old wounds have not healed.
- Symptoms are confused with underlying causes.

Planning. Developing a strategy and action plan.

- Choose one of the nine available strategies or a blend of strategies, congruent with the situation, along with a backup plan.
- Mutually agree with the other party on a time and place to explore differences and a time frame in which to do it.
- Decide how to monitor the process and what the consequences will be of failure to live up to any agreement.

Implementation. Carry out the plan.

- Maintain a tone of mutual respect and goodwill.
- Consider putting any agreement in writing.

Follow-up. After agreement has been reached:

- Monitor results to verify that the agreement is being honored.
- If the agreement is not being honored, learn why and then take corrective action.
- Reinforce behavior that supports the agreement.
- Learn from each experience with conflict and disagreement.

USES OF THE CONCEPTS

Organizational change—whether a program of continuous improvement, total quality management, process reengineering, empowerment, or simply a change in a bookkeeping system—creates personal vulnerability. Change threatens existing competence, control, status, and privilege. Therefore, it is not unusual for people to have different views of a proposed change or of how to implement changes. One key to implementing change successfully is dealing constructively with people who hold different views. Therefore, the concepts presented here are of value to both organizational consultants and managers.

When consultants and trainers introduce the nine-strategies model to clients and seminar participants in a conflict-management context, their presentations are more relevant. As trainees practice using the principles, strategies, and process for managing conflict and disagreement constructively, results will manifest as better teamwork, improved communication, and more creative solutions.

References

Blake, R.R. & Mouton, J.S. (1964). *The Managerial Grid.* Houston, TX: Gulf.

Kindler, H.S. (1983). The art of managing differences. *Training & Development Journal, 37*(1), 27-32.

Kindler, H.S. (1994). *Management of differences inventory* (rev. ed.). Pacific Palisades, CA: Center for Management Effectiveness.

Herbert S. Kindler, Ph.D., is the director of the Center for Management Effectiveness, Pacific Palisades, California, and is professor emeritus of management and organization at Loyola Marymount University. He is the author or coauthor of five books, the author of several workbooks and educational films, and the developer of the Management of Differences Inventory. *Dr. Kindler's past experience as the CEO of an engineering firm enriches his international training and consulting activities.*

USING EXPERIENTIAL LEARNING TO IMPROVE QUALITY

Ellie S. Browner and Robert C. Preziosi

Abstract: Quality improvement is an issue that is addressed by teams, not individuals; yet many workers do not possess the skills necessary to work effectively in teams. Experiential-learning methods such as games, simulations, and instrumentation are particularly appropriate for team learning. The authors offer a detailed explanation of how to select games, simulations, and instruments that are particularly appropriate for quality-improvement training. They suggest that the first step in selection is determining the role of the team itself—to improve steadily, at a rate of 5 to 15 percent annually (a "continuous-improvement team"), or to achieve a breakthrough improvement of 50 to 90 percent (a "quality-breakthrough team").

The kinds of activities and training topics that are appropriate for team building with both kinds of teams are discussed. Subsequently, the authors suggest how to conduct activities, covering the four major phases of preparing, introducing, experiencing, and debriefing. The authors conclude with a pictorial representation of their own model for using activities, which is based on these four phases.

The 1995 Annual: Volume 1, Training.
Copyright © 1995 by Pfeiffer & Company, San Diego, CA.

Quality improvement, like most other issues in today's organizations, is addressed by teams, not individuals. Yet many workers—especially those in the U.S., who were brought up in a culture that rewards individuality—lack the necessary skills to resolve issues effectively in a team setting.

As Rogers (Myers, 1989) states, "For 16 years of schooling, students are told, 'Keep to yourself. Do your own work.' Now, for the first time...trainees are told, 'Here's the problem. The four of you must solve it together.' "

Consequently, for the practitioner of human resource development (HRD), the challenge of implementing a quality program in an organization frequently involves changing not only the culture of that organization but also the culture of learning itself. The practitioner must begin to think in terms of "learning teams" whose members have the potential to think and act collectively to solve an organization's quality problems.

Learning must be viewed as a collaborative experience—a team experience—rather than an individualistic one. Team learning, according to Senge (1990), is the process of aligning and developing the capacity of team members to create the results that those members truly desire.

Experiential-learning methods such as games, simulations, and instrumentation are particularly appropriate for team learning. A wide variety of experiential tools are available in many formats, and practitioners involved with quality-improvement programs must become knowledgeable about these tools.

DEFINITIONS

In order to build a framework for the use and applicability of experiential-learning methods that will help to improve teamwork and quality, the practitioner needs to become familiar with the definitions of a number of terms (Table 1). Following the table is a more detailed explanation of these terms.

Term	Definition
Game	An activity in which two or more participants compete, usually for fun.
Simulation	An interactive, dynamic learning experience that mirrors a real-life situation (through their decisions and actions, participants can effect changes or be affected by those changes).
Simulation Game	An activity that combines the characteristics of a game and a simulation (a game-based simulation).
Instrument	A paper-and-pencil device used to assess or take an inventory of oneself.

Table 1. A Guide to Terms Used in Experiential-Learning Methods

Games

Games are brief, usually not more than thirty minutes each in duration. They are characteristically inexpensive; when the practitioner develops a game himself or herself, that game often can be included in a training session at no cost.

Most games involve participants physically or psychologically, causing them to think, act, and/or laugh. When a game is matched appropriately to the training objectives, it provides a low-risk, highly successful learning experience. Even those purchased commercially have high learning impact when used properly.

Most games can be modified easily to fit a training objective without changing their original flavor. Games may be used as icebreakers, to "warm up" the group and grab attention and to encourage participation; to provide a vivid, visual illustration of technical-skill building; to reinforce learning by providing an opportunity to "test" the transfer of learning through feedback; or to add vitality to the closure of a session and to link the transfer of learning to the real world. Sometimes a game may be used simply to energize the group or as a stress releaser for a particularly long or tedious training session.

Simulations

A pure simulation does not involve the competition and closure that are typical of a game. Simulations are generally used to provide hands-on experience when participants are implementing new equipment or computer software or new systems (as in quality-improvement projects). Simulations, when properly designed, are as close to the real world as imaginable.

Simulation Games

A simulation game combines the elements of a game (competition, objectives, and closure) and those of a simulation. There are thousands of simulation games in use today, most falling into one or more of the categories shown in Table 2.

Category	Description
Gamut Running	Resembles the format of a board game. Used for all types of content: technical, managerial, sales, etc.
Allocation Game	Involves allocation of resources, budget, or power/influence.
Group Interaction	Exposes participants to a new point of view or way of thinking.
General-System Game	Presents a complex model of the total system of an organization.

Table 2. Categories of Simulation Games

Advantages of Games and Simulations

Games and simulations combine real-life tasks with important information or insights connected with those tasks to provide participants with skills or knowledge that ordinarily might take weeks, months, or even years to obtain. When a game or simulation deals with continuous quality improvement, the discoveries made by participants can clearly demonstrate the positive bottom-line value of training to the organization. Also, participants are required to work together collaboratively, just as they must in their own work teams to improve quality.

Disadvantages of Games and Simulations

Some participants may perceive games and simulations as frivolous compared to traditional instructional methods. Often the participants who have such perceptions are accustomed to the traditional roles of teacher and learner in which the learner passively absorbs whatever information the teacher dispenses.

> *Resistance can be diverted by emphasizing real-life applications.*

These participants often expect to leave a training session with a notebook crammed full of notes and a serious case of writer's cramp. When they have participated in games or simulations instead, they may leave feeling frustrated and even angry, believing that they have not learned anything.

An HRD practitioner who is skilled in group facilitation can divert some of this resistance by fully explaining the roles of the instructor and the learner, by ensuring that all participants actively participate in the experience, and by emphasizing the real-life application of the learning. The practitioner should stress the important link between collaboration in the learning environment and collaboration in the workplace.

Instruments

Use of instruments is popular in many quality-improvement programs since they are based on quantifiable data, just as quality improvement must be.

Instruments offer many advantages. They provide an easy way to teach theory and concepts and usually produce involvement and interest. Participants receive insightful information about themselves and their teammates through instruments.

Also, when instruments are used repeatedly over time, they can measure change. In addition, instruments can provide useful information about individual potential within groups. Finally, their use demonstrates the value of openness in communication, which is essential in the quest for improvement in quality.

Certain disadvantages are also incurred with the use of instruments. Some participants fear that their scores will be made public and used against them (Bowen, Hall, Lewicki, & Hall, 1989):

> This is a real and legitimate fear and should be honored. Only ask people to share their scores in small groups and with people they trust. Don't ask people to share their scores in large groups unless they are willing. (p. 20).

It is possible to chart people's scores without identifying which scores belong to whom. Also, it is important that the practitioner share his or her own score with the group; doing so models openness and trust.

Some participants may question whether an instrument is meaningful. This difficulty may be overcome by linking the instrument to real-life examples. Also, the practitioner should be prepared to explore any data that tend to contradict the ways in which participants perceive themselves.

Finally, the practitioner should be prepared to discuss the reliability and validity of the instrument. If he or she is not prepared to respond adequately to participants' doubts about an instrument, that instrument should not be used. By being prepared, the practitioner demonstrates an important principle of quality improvement.

COURSE DESIGN AND LESSON PLANNING

Strategic course design and careful lesson planning are key elements in selecting experiential-learning techniques that are appropriate for quality-improvement training in a collaborative learning environment. Both are driven by participant needs and program objectives. Each, however, requires a different strategy to ensure that a successful transfer of learning occurs.

Course Design

During the course-design phase, the designer concentrates on the "big picture." At this macro level, he or she is concerned with a number of issues:

- The development of learning objectives and desired outcomes;
- Time concerns such as development and scheduling;
- Costs;
- The number of participants;
- Facility logistics;
- Cultural and diversity issues;

- The availability and talents of trainers and instructors; and
- Compliance with mandated legislation, such as the Americans with Disabilities Act (ADA).

Of these, the development of learning objectives is the most critical.[1] Learning objectives fall into three general categories: skills, knowledge, and attitudes. Table 3 illustrates the relationship between learning objectives and the appropriate use of games, simulations, and instruments.

Category	Focus of Learning	Games	Simulations	Instruments
Skills	Physical manipulation of equipment/objects	●	●	
Knowledge	Cognitive or mental processes	●		●
Attitudes	Perceptions, attitudes, behavioral changes	●		●

Table 3. The Relationship Between Learning Objectives and Games, Simulations, and Instruments

Lesson Planning

Lesson planning represents the micro level of course design. A lesson plan or "blueprint" is developed to keep the learning on track and focused.

For each activity that is considered and selected, the planner must take certain steps:

- Assess whether the activity will build and create a collaborative learning experience;
- Determine how the activity will be introduced;
- Develop appropriate ways to segue into and out of the activity (linking the activity appropriately and smoothly to the one that precedes it and the one that follows it);
- Test whether the learning involved in the activity fits appropriately with the course objectives and whether the activity needs to be customized to meet those objectives;
- Take an inventory of the equipment/handouts required to conduct the activity (furniture, game pieces, observer sheets, work sheets, etc.);
- Develop questions for processing and debriefing the activity;

---

[1] Note that team development of the objectives mirrors quality values.

- Test the logical sequence and timing of the activity; and
- Ensure that a transfer of learning will take place.

SELECTING ACTIVITIES

Continuous-Improvement Teams Versus Breakthrough Teams

An important first step in researching and determining the appropriateness of activities for improving teamwork and quality is to determine the role of the team itself in an organization's quality-enhancement efforts: Is the purpose of the team to build a continuous-improvement environment (a steady process of improvement of 5, 10, or 15 percent annually) or to achieve a breakthrough (a dramatic gain of 50- to 90-percent improvement)?

The characteristics of continuous-improvement (CI) teams and breakthrough teams are quite different (Hay, 1992):

> Simply stated, the goal of a CI process is to get as many people as possible involved in a total quality (TQ) effort, and to achieve real but incremental improvement as a result. The goal of a breakthrough process is to achieve quick dramatic quality improvement in an area that's critically important to the business. (p. 12)

Table 4 compares the roles of continuous-improvement and breakthrough teams.

CHARACTERISTIC	CONTINUOUS-IMPROVEMENT TEAM	QUALITY-BREAKTHROUGH TEAM
Team Profile	Natural work group	Cross-functional team
Goal	Long-term improvement	Two to three business targets per year
Life Cycle	Ongoing (indefinite)	Four to six months
Number of Team Members	Approximately twelve to fifteen	Five to seven
Organizational Structure	Committee structure (operating with a defined set of procedures and processes)	Project-management structure
Leadership Role	Shared	Formal leader, with task-specific skill and/or influential leadership style
Return on Investment	Slow process/results	Rapid results
Task/Project Selection	Group selects improvement targets	Improvement targets assigned

Table 4. Roles of Continuous-Improvement and Breakthrough Teams

Team-Building Training

Both continuous-improvement and breakthrough teams require team-building sessions, and it is imperative that trust be established as the central thread of such sessions. According to Hay (1992), one "...kind of training both [continuous improvement and breakthrough] teams need—and the kind they never get in many companies—is team-building; that is, training on how to work effectively in a team environment."

However, the specific content of the team-building sessions and the activities used are distinctly different for the two types of teams:

1. *Team-building strategies for a continuous-improvement team.* These strategies should emphasize long-term team development; shared commitment; a quality focus on data-collection techniques, problem solving, change, and customer identification; and a general understanding of statistical process control (SPC) methods.

2. *Team-building strategies for a breakthrough team.* These strategies should provide members with the skills to develop their team at an accelerated rate as well as the skills to bring positive closure to their team experience at the appropriate time. Also included should be activities that build trust across cross-functional lines as well as activities that build specific skills to address performance problems, project management, and advanced SPC measures.

Team building fosters not only valuable skills and attitudes but also creativity. A team tends to be more creative than one person working alone. Thus, any continuous-improvement program benefits from the addition of team-building efforts. In fact, the Massachusetts Institute of Technology (MIT) Commission on Industrial Competitiveness has identified creativity as the most important factor in efforts to gain competitive advantage.

According to Robert W. Galvin (1991) of Motorola Corporation, creativity is the missing ingredient in many quality-training programs. Galvin contends that "creative thinking is essential to the problem solving factors of getting quality up to a level of perfection. We [organizations] can't do that without optimal creative thinking."

Group-Dynamics Training

Successful quality teams must understand and be comfortable with the small-group process (see, for example, Bradford, 1978; Dimock, 1987). Team members must be aware of the developmental cycles of group dynamics and the ways in which individual behavior patterns impact both relationships and work in small-group settings.

Topics to Include in Training for Quality Teams

An article in *Training & Development* by Ted Cocheu (1992) suggests topics to include in training for quality teams. Cocheu divides these training topics into three categories (see Figure 1) according to the intended participants: managers, team members, and team leaders.

Topic	Managers	Members	Leaders
Building participative environments	●		
Leading versus managing	●		
Trust	●	●	●
Delegating	●		●
Coaching teams	●		●
Self-empowerment		●	●
Meeting management		●	●
Identifying team types		●	●
Team formation	●		●
Team development	●	●	●
Group processing		●	●
Problem solving		●	●
Decision making		●	●
Seven quality tools*		●	●
Project planning		●	●
Gaining support			●
Conflict resolution		●	●
Creativity	●	●	●
Communication	●	●	●
Basic SPC		●	●
Visioning and goal setting	●	●	●

Figure 1. Training Topics for Quality Teams

*The seven quality tools are brainstorming; cause-and-effect diagrams; checklists; histograms; Pareto charts; scattergrams; and other kinds of charts, such as run charts. For additional readings on the seven quality tools, see Hodgetts (1993), Chang & Niedzwiecki (1994), and Eshelman & Cooksey (1992).

CONDUCTING ACTIVITIES

A crucial factor in the success of using a collaboration-based activity in training a quality team is the skill with which the practitioner conducts the experience. All such activities share four major phases: preparing, introducing, experiencing, and debriefing.

Preparing

When using an activity in training a quality team, the practitioner must be organized, prepared, and completely familiar with the activity design. By preparing adequately, the practitioner models an emphasis on quality.

Proper preparation includes developing a thorough understanding of the following:

- How the activity fits the instructional needs of the participants;
- How it helps to meet the objectives of the training session; and
- How it coordinates with the overall goals, objectives, and culture of the organization.

For instance, if the participants function in a health-care environment, then the activity should model a health-care system. Similarly, if the participants are from the banking industry, then the activity should mirror a banking environment. If the purpose is to train trainers, then the participants should be able to see the relevance of the activity to their own training settings.

Finally, the trainer must be prepared in terms of practical issues, such as scheduling, arranging meeting space, and collecting materials, as well as in terms of contingencies that might occur, such as interruptions or difficulties that will need to be dealt with.

1. *Interruptions.* Interruptions can seriously disrupt learning and should be avoided. For this reason the practitioner may want to meet with the participants off-site or at least in an area that is separate from their normal meeting space. In this way phone calls, requests from coworkers, and other interruptions may be forestalled.

2. *Difficulties.* One excellent way to become familiar with possible difficulties—such as discussions that stray from the goals of the experience or high affect—is to share the activity design in advance with other practitioners. This use of networking can provide valuable insights that will help in preparing for what might occur during an activity.

Introducing

In introducing the activity, the practitioner should clarify his or her own role as well as the responsibilities of the participants. It is also important for the practitioner to set the tone of the learning experience by creating an atmosphere of trust with and among the participants.

To create such an environment, the practitioner should stress the following points:

- Any and all learning from the upcoming activity is legitimate and valuable;

- All reactions (both thoughts and feelings) generated by the activity will be honored; and

- The participants' actions during the activity will not be judged or held against them in any way.

In addition, the practitioner should explain the purpose of the activity, should provide enough information for the participants to proceed on their own, and should then "step back" so that the participants can experience the learning. All of these behaviors are consistent with the tenets of quality improvement.

> *Participants should be allowed to think, act, decide, and learn for themselves.*

Experiencing

Participants should be allowed to think, act, decide, and learn for themselves. The trainer's primary responsibility during the experiencing phase is to observe and evaluate the process and to provide support, understanding, and enthusiasm. By meeting this responsibility, the practitioner demonstrates the values of quality improvement.

If subgroups are formed, it is useful to "visit" each subgroup briefly to monitor the activity and to ensure that the participants are carrying it out as specified. It is not a good idea to leave the room for any length of time; participants may need advice or clarification of a task. Also, the practitioner may be called on to ameliorate frustration or to mediate a disagreement.

Debriefing

At the conclusion of an activity, the practitioner facilitates a discussion. One trap that practitioners sometimes fall into is that of allotting only a few brief minutes to debrief. Bowen et al. (1982) point out that an activity is not worth doing if there is not sufficient time for adequate processing and subsequent discussion. A thorough debriefing discussion generally takes fifteen to twenty minutes and should be guided by specific questions to the participants that relate closely to the goals of the activity.

Much of the learning from an activity takes place and is recognized by participants during the concluding discussion. Without adequate debriefing, participants do not see the experience as meaningful, relevant, or valuable.

A SAMPLE ACTIVITY

An example of using team or collaborative learning in a quality-improvement effort is provided in an activity entitled "Poster Designs: Learning the Characteristics of Quality Measures," whose participants are members of three or more functional teams.

Lecturette

The activity begins with a lecturette on the characteristics of good quality measures:

- *Timeliness*—A measure that is *timely* provides data quickly enough so that corrective action can be taken on a minor difficulty before it becomes a major problem.
- *Validity*—A measure that is *valid* provides data that show actual changes in quality dimensions;
- *Cost-effectiveness*—A measure that is *cost-effective* is one that represents the least costly approach possible; and
- *Usefulness*—A measure that is *useful* is not only easy to use but also acceptable to those who must apply it in the process of making decisions.

The practitioner presents examples of these measures and then allows time for questions.

Subgroup Task: Poster Design

Next the participants are organized into subgroups, each of which includes members from all functions represented.

Each subgroup is given newsprint sheets and as many felt-tipped markers as there are subgroup members. (The markers should be different colors.) Each subgroup is instructed to create a poster depicting the four characteristics: timeliness, validity, cost-effectiveness, and usefulness. The practitioner tells the subgroups that they have thirty minutes to complete the task and then monitors the task work to ensure that all subgroup members are participating actively.

After each poster has been completed, it is signed by all of the members who created it.

Poster Review and Discussion

The posters are taped to the walls. The participants are instructed to move around the room reviewing all of the posters.

Subsequently, the practitioner leads a discussion about the poster content. The following questions may be useful during this discussion:

- What do the posters tell you about the various characteristics of quality measures?

- What did you learn as a result of the process of illustrating these measures?

- How will you use what you have learned during this activity to improve quality in your own team?

- How can you share what you have learned with other people in the organization who have not participated in this activity?

Conclusion/Options

The session may be concluded at this time, or the practitioner may continue the discussion by dealing with another quality-related issue:

- Creative behavior;

- Conflict management;

- Communication; or

- Problem solving.

Another option is to reconfigure the subgroups according to functions and have each subgroup develop a set of measures for its own functional activities.

PIED MODEL FOR USING ACTIVITIES

Deming (1986) advocates the use of a Shewhart Plan-Do-Check-Act model to ensure a continuous-improvement cycle. Shewhart developed the concept of cyclical continuous improvement for his study titled "Statistical Method from the Viewpoint of Quality Control." Deming presented the model in Japan in 1950 as the Shewhart cycle. "It went into immediate use in Japan under the name of the Deming cycle, and so it has been called ever since" (p. 88). Figure 2 presents an adaptation, the Prepare-Introduce-Experience-Debrief (PIED) model, which may be followed to ensure continuous improvement in the process of using activities in a training setting. Use of the PIED model supports the relationship between quality and learning.

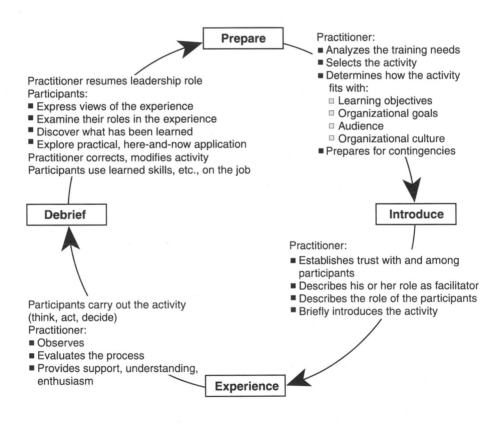

Figure 2. Preparing-Introducing-Experiencing-Debriefing (PIED) Model

Conclusion

It is tempting to an HRD practitioner to develop a repertoire of familiar training activities and to cling exclusively to these activities. But if we practitioners are to be role models for change in the quality movement, we must take the lead in the training setting by using new and creative activities for improving quality through teamwork.

References and Bibliography

Bowen, D.D., Hall, D.T., Lewicki, R.J., & Hall, F.S. (1989). *Instructor's manual: Experiences in management and organizational behavior* (2nd ed.). New York: John Wiley & Sons.

Bradford, L.P. (Ed.). (1978). *Group development* (2nd ed.). San Diego, CA: Pfeiffer & Company.

Chang, R.Y., & Niedzwiecki, M.E. (1994). *Continuous improvement tools* (Vol. 1). Irvine, CA: Richard Chang Associates, Inc.

Cocheu, T. (1992, May). Training with quality. *Training and Development,* pp. 23-32.

Deming, W.E. (1986). *Out of crisis* (17th ed.). Cambridge, MA: Massachusetts Institute of Technology, Center for Advanced Engineering Study.

Dimock, H.G. (1987). *Groups: Leadership and group development.* San Diego, CA: Pfeiffer & Company.

Eshelman, D., & Cooksey, C. (1992, April). Quality: The quality toolbox [Special issue]. *Training,* pp. 19-30.

Galvin, R.W. (Speaker). (1991). *The case for quality: Economic and classroom implications* (Cassette Recording No. SB-B01). High Ridge, MO: Network Communications.

Gitlow, H. (1990). *Planning for quality, productivity, and competitive position* (pp. 35-36). Homewood, Il: Dow Jones-Irwin.

Haslam, E.L. (1990). The case of simulation. In R.B. Frantzreb (Ed.), *Training and development handbook: 1991 Edition* (pp.6.16-6.19). Englewood Cliffs, NJ: Prentice-Hall.

Hay, E.J. (1992, November). Continuous improvement: Don't expect breakthrough results. *The Quality Observer,* pp. 1, 12.

Hodgetts, R.M. (1993). *Blueprints for continuous improvement: Lessons from the Baldrige winners.* New York: American Management Association.

Keiser, T.C., & Seeler, J.H. (1987). Games and simulations. In R.L. Craig (Ed.), *Training and development handbook: A guide to human resource development* (3rd ed.) (pp. 456-468). New York: McGraw-Hill.

Myers, W. (1989, May/June). Teamwork scores corporate victories. *Women in Business,* pp. 14-19.

Senge, P. (1990). *The fifth discipline.* New York: Doubleday.

Ellie S. Browner is the assistant director of the Center for Management Development at Florida International University. She manages all publicly offered certificate programs and designs the curriculum for certificate programs for human resource and health-care professionals. She has given train-the-trainer and supervisory-skills workshops, emphasizing total quality management, team building, managing change, and adventure-based learning. Ms. Browner has been active in the Miami, Broward, and Dade chapters of ASTD and is a past president of the American Business Women's Association. She is the coauthor of the 1991 Southeast Florida Salary Survey for Training Professionals.

Robert C. Preziosi, Ph.D., is the associate dean of and a professor of management education in the School of Business and Entrepreneurship at Nova University in Fort Lauderdale, Florida. He is also the president of Management Associates, a consulting firm. He has worked as a human resources director, a line manager, and a leadership-training administrator and has consulted with all levels of management in many organizations, including American Express, the Department of Health and Human Services, John Alden Life Insurance, Siemens, and a large number of hospitals and banks. Dr. Preziosi has been training trainers since the 1970s; his areas of interest include leadership, adult learning, and all aspects of management and executive development. In 1984 he was given the Outstanding Contribution to HRD Award by the American Society for Training and Development (ASTD); in 1990 he received the Torch Award, the highest leadership award that ASTD gives.

THE CHANGING ORGANIZATION: NEW CHALLENGES FOR HRD PROFESSIONALS AND MANAGERS

Robert William Lucas

Abstract: In the past few decades, dramatic economic and technological changes have led to equally dramatic changes in the business environment. One resulting challenge for the HRD professional is finding and hiring employees who have basic business skills. Another is ongoing job training for managers and employees. New technologies and process reengineering require job retraining and motivational training. As the educational system is less able to provide the requisite knowledge and skills for workers and as the work force becomes more diverse, organizations have to spend larger portions of their budgets on training.

One way in which HRD professionals can help to meet this need is to establish alliances and partnerships with other businesses, governmental agencies, and educational institutions. In addition, HRD professionals need to be able to conduct business-needs analyses as well as training-needs analyses; they need to be able to envision trends, guide organizational change, and train people at all levels of the organization to deal with the shifting requirements of the organizational environment.

In the past decades, there have been dramatic changes in technology, the international arena, and workplace demographics, all of which have greatly affected the ways in which organizations do business. There have been continual changes in society, the economy, and managerial roles. Changes in organizational structures resulting from mergers, consolidations, and expansions have become the rule, rather than the exception. Not since the industrial revolution has the creation of new industries, organizations, products, and services been so pervasive and so rapid in response to change.

CHANGES OVER THE PAST DECADES

Toffler (1990) observed that following World War II, the United States came to realize an age of expansion and improvement unparalleled by most countries. Having survived the war with its industry and borders intact, a steady period of growth began and lasted until the 1960s. Along with the Soviet Union, whose desire for technology plunged it into a period of near chaotic change in 1989, the U.S. dominated world power.

During that period, employees were content to work for one company for most of their adult lives and be rewarded with "retirement nest eggs." The U.S. became the dominant world force in areas of production and service. Because U.S. companies did not fear foreign competition, production slowed—compared to other countries—and service began to decline. The U.S. went from being one of the world's largest creditors to being its largest debtor nation in a few decades.

In the 1970s, the contentment of being part of the "Great Society" turned to fear of oil shortages and unemployment. Events were set into motion that led to a major recession in which: a) more financial institutions failed than at any time since the depression; b) bankruptcy declarations became commonplace; c) employers began seeking solutions to a changing work ethic and diverse work force; and d) the quality of products and services declined.

Peters (1987) found that during the 1980s, the U.S. gross national product (GNP) slipped behind that of Japan, West Germany, Switzerland, and several other European nations. During the same period, the U.S. service industry lost most of the $41 billion in positive trade balance it once held.

To deal with and survive this shift, organizations began campaigns to motivate and reeducate employees and the public. They began to adopt a proactive approach to counter what was perceived as a downward spiral for U.S. business and to attack rather than defend the status quo. Slogans such as Chrysler's "The Pride Is Back" and Ford's "Quality Is Job One" exemplified this approach.

The state of the economy and lack of distribution of appropriate knowledge experienced in the 1990s are not solely the result of lack of forethought on the part of industry leaders of the past. Many things have contributed to these problems. Still, experts believe it will take more than a change in economics to correct the problems. Toffler (1990) believes for example, that neither Keynesian nor Monetarist economics alone can increase global effectiveness, curb unemployment, or reverse change.

With all the turbulence occurring in the business environment, managers of the future, according to Drucker (1980), will have to develop "strategies for tomorrow, strategies that anticipate where the greatest changes are likely to occur and what they are likely to be, strategies that enable a business...to take advantage of new realities" (p. 4).

WHAT IS NEEDED?

The challenges of a fast-changing environment include the need for constantly updated personnel training. McElwain (1991) suggests that as much as 42 percent (50 million) of the workers currently employed in the U.S. are in need of additional training to develop them on personal and professional levels and to enhance their attitudes toward work. In current dollar figures, this new training, coupled with existing training, could have a total annual cost of $45 billion.

Traditionally, corporate leaders have eliminated training when budget cuts were necessary because training was viewed as a cost that did not provide tangible returns. Recently, this view has been changing through the efforts of the American Society for Training and Development, the National Society for Performance and Instruction, the Society of Human Resource Managers, some educational institutions, and legions of human resource and training practitioners. As a result of their efforts, many organizations are dedicating larger percentages of their budgets to personnel procurement and development in efforts to select and train employees who can deal with the complex issues and technologies of today.

Additionally, more managers realize that their employees need training and education. They are also investing sizeable amounts of time, energy, and resources to conduct training needs analyses prior to implementing training programs. Through this impetus, employees are learning new skills that allow them to perform more effectively in their new or reshaped work settings and to produce quality products and/or services. A Japanese axiom succinctly summarizes the benefits of training: "Quality control starts with training and ends with training."

According to a joint study conducted by the U.S. Department of Labor (DOL) and the American Society for Training and Development (ASTD) (Carnevale, Gainer, & Meltzer, 1990), many of the largest companies in the U.S. currently spend about 2 percent of their payrolls on training and development. Even so, the study recommends that more money be dedicated to employee training—possibly as much as 4 percent. This proposed amount would equal an annual increase of $14 billion for formal training and would include 10 to 15 percent more employees. Although this sum may seem large, it is only about one-tenth of the amount that employers spend yearly on facilities and technology.

THE NEW EMPHASIS ON TRAINING

A lack of updated training practices has created myriad dysfunctions in organizational systems. For years, the U.S. has depended too heavily on an overburdened academic and vocational training system to pump newly qualified applicants into the job market. A great many of these applicants do not have the basic skills needed by employers or the knowledge, skills, and attitudes needed to deal with technical and service issues. According to the ASTD-DOL study, employers are requiring more of their employees in the way of technical knowledge, basic skills (reading, writing, learning) and personal-relations skills. Because many applicants do not possess these skills, employers are buying or developing training programs to teach them. In addition, they are spending billions of dollars each year to train their managers and supervisors in order to better equip them to cope with the challenges of a diverse work force and a changing work environment.

Training and retraining have become paramount issues with most employers and employees because of their desire to stay in step with economic and technical change and to remain competitive. As more people acknowledge this trend, more money is likely to be put into providing training. Carnevale et al (1990) estimate that in 1990, 39 million individuals received 1.3 billion hours of employer-sponsored formal and informal training at a cost of over $200 billion or 1 to 2 percent of payroll costs. This amount is more than the gross national product of many nations and is more than all expenditures per year for education in the U.S.—primary grades through college.

FORMING PARTNERSHIPS

Organizations in the U.S. are striving to regain the position that they held formerly in the world market. They are doing this by developing new ways of thinking and new management systems and by educating, training, or retraining their employees.

In addition to providing in-house training, organizations are going outside their own business environments to establish partnerships with other businesses, governmental agencies, and educational institutions. As they recognize that they and the schools systems cannot train all employees adequately, they are looking for greater resources and expertise elsewhere.

In 1990, the national headquarters of the American Automobile Association (AAA) demonstrated the value of such a partnership by entering into a joint venture with the State of Florida. AAA experienced massive change when the national headquarters relocated with several hundred employees from Virginia to Florida, moved its Florida district office from Miami, hired over three hundred new employees, and changed from a typewriter-driven to a computerized environment.

Partnerships offer access to greater resources and expertise.

As part of the relocation program, AAA and the State of Florida formed a training partnership in which the state, through Seminole Community College, provided a $150,000 matching-fund, economic-development grant. This grant helped provide thousands of hours of training in the form of new-employee orientation and management, supervisory, and technical training. The result was a continuance of excellent customer service at the same time that AAA upgraded job skills and provided education in its corporate values and philosophy.

SHAPING NEW ROLES

In future U.S. organizations, managers and human resource development (HRD) professionals will be responsible for eliciting their employees' full potential. The latter group will have to function in a number of roles to attain organizational goals. These roles will vary, depending on immediate need, but will primarily revolve around the managers' ability to recruit, hire, train, coach, counsel, and evaluate employees. HRD professionals will have to prepare managers by creating valid business-needs assessments. They will also have to design or procure and then deliver training programs to teach managers the required skills. Additionally, training will be needed to reinforce previous learnings; to teach supervisors and managers to understand

and value diversity and change; to introduce new policies, procedures, and technologies; and to assist managers in their own professional growth.

Bridges (1980) suggests dividing training into three categories:

- Seminars for top management in leading an organization through change,

- Workshops and individual coaching for middle managers and supervisors in managing people in transition, and

- Workshops in making change work for individuals who are most at risk because of changes.

"By taking a top-down approach," Bridges concludes, "a better likelihood of success exists."

For HRD personnel to be effective in the future, they must understand their roles and those of managers as leaders in reshaping their organizations. They also must be able to envision trends; formulate strategies to address the needs of their organizations, employees, and customers; and become advocates of change or act as change agents to carry out the changes. As London (1988) puts it, "To be effective, human resource professionals need to understand change from the perspectives of the leaders and managers they support as well as from their own perspective."

THE NEW ORGANIZATION

The changes taking place in business have forced organizations to reevaluate and modify their human resource systems and the ways in which employees are managed. More than ever, organizations need to apply sound management practices to help attract, guide, motivate, educate, and retain talented employees.

Organizations must develop strategies to address many issues. All members of an organization will have to understand that the philosophy of "business as usual" does not work in a frequently changing environment. Organizations must examine demographic changes, such as a more diverse work force, while managers and human resource personnel must actively involve the diverse groups in finding valid solutions to their issues. Managers and HRD professionals must work together to facilitate change and, at the same time, to reduce the resulting anxiety for employees and the organization. To compensate for the shrinking middle-management force and to aid employees who are caught up in change, employers will have to offer opportunities for employees to maximize their individual potential through employee empowerment and education.

Organizational change is pervasive and ongoing. To capitalize on change, organizational leaders and HRD professionals need to be more proactive. If changes are planned and implemented effectively, and if they are supported by appropriate training, the results may be measured in terms of greater productivity, higher morale, increased quality, and reduced costs.

References

Bridges, W. (1980). *Transitions: Making sense of life's changes.* Reading, MA: Addison-Wesley.

Carnevale, A., Gainer, L., and Meltzer, A. (1990). *Workplace basics: The skills employers want.* San Francisco: Jossey-Bass.

Drucker, P. (1980). *Managing in turbulent times.* New York: Harper.

London, M. (1988). *Change agents: New roles and innovation strategies for human resources professionals.* San Francisco: Jossey-Bass.

McElwain, J. (1991, March). The training gap. *Training and Development Journal,* pp. 9-10.

Peters, T. (1987). *Thriving on chaos: Handbook for a management revolution.* New York: Knopf.

Toffler, A. (1991). *Powershift.* New York: Bantam.

Robert William (Bob) Lucas is the Training Manager at the National Headquarters of the American Automobile Association in Heathrow, Florida. For the past twenty-two years, he has conducted training in profit, nonprofit, military, government, consulting, and volunteer environments. His areas of expertise include management and training program development, interpersonal communication, adult learning, customer service, and employee development. Mr. Lucas has served on the board of ASTD in Washington, D.C. and in Orlando, Florida, where he is currently President. He has authored several books, including Coaching Skills: A Guide for Supervisors, Effective Interpersonal Skills, *and* Training Skills for Supervisors.

GENERAL INCLUSION GROUPS VERSUS INDIVIDUAL INITIATIVE NETWORKS

Stanley M. Herman

Abstract: In the training and organization development (OD) professions, an overemphasis on systems
and teams may well have obscured the importance of
developing individuals. This article explores the current imbalance in perspective. It examines the uses
and limitations of typical organizational groups.
These are identified as "general inclusion groups"
(GIGs), which include groups that are based on the
principle of participation by everybody involved in the
activity or issue being addressed. Subsequently, the
composition and functions of the GIGs are contrasted
with those of "individual initiative networks" (IINs),
configurations of goal-driven individuals and their
supporters. The power of the IIN is the vision, initiative, and determination of individuals working in voluntary combination to achieve a particular goal.
Examples are given of the kinds of things that IINs can
achieve.

The article concludes with a discussion of the role
of HRD professionals in creating, training, and supporting effective organizational groups without ignor-
ing or shortchanging the power and potential of the
individual.

T here is a distinct possibility that the organization development (OD) and training professions have been seduced by the "systems viewpoint" and have lost sight of the importance of developing and training autonomous individuals. Over the last decade, most of the best minds and talents in human resource development (HRD) have been increasingly focused on large-scale change and employee-involvement groups. This has been accompanied by heavy concentration on the development and delivery of mass training aimed at changing organizational cultures. There has been relatively little concentration on the development and facilitation of the individual, as pathfinder, initiator, implementer, or even as an effective member of a work group or network—Gifford Pinchot's work on "intrapreneuring" being the exception.

The case to be made in this article is not antagonistic to systems thinking or group training. It is quite clear that these orientations serve valuable purposes. However, if our preoccupation with them becomes exclusive, if we forget that all systems are concocted abstractions and that all groups are composed of individual members, we perpetuate a potentially dangerous imbalance. Our too general championing of these approaches may be obscuring some important realities. These are as follows:

1. Preoccupation with large-scale systems has encouraged a tendency among training and OD people to use "cookbook" interventions and techniques that are often inappropriate for the organization. Concurrently, many HRD people are neglecting the basic skills of group process, diagnosis, readiness assessment, and political acumen that would make their efforts more relevant and functional.

2. An indiscriminate advocacy of employee-involvement teams as the cure for what ails organizations is dysfunctional. HRD and OD specialists need to recognize that different working configurations are effective for different purposes and at different times. This includes understanding that developing the potential contribution of exceptional individuals and key leaders is essential for surviving and flourishing in a highly competitive environment.

3. There are two central purposes of HRD: the improvement of organizational effectiveness and the development of individual growth and competence.

The significant contributions of OD and training to organizational effectiveness have been increasingly recognized by management. A number of HRD professionals have gained access to top management. They facilitate strategic planning sessions, implement company-wide quality and customer-orientation programs, help develop more rapid product-development cycles, and conduct large-scale employee-involvement efforts. HRD managers, like most managers, enjoy being involved in large, important issues, which usually translates to involvement with systems and groups—the bigger, the more important.

Programs designed by successful HRD professionals have served as models for others who, understandably, want to emulate their success. Unfortunately, attempts to transfer principles and methods directly from one organization to another—as though they were universally applicable—have frequently resulted in frustration and failure.

THE GENERAL INCLUSION GROUP

General inclusion groups (GIGs) are formations such as quality circles, problem-solving groups, semiautonomous work groups, and employee-involvement groups. These formations are generally based on the principle of participation by everybody involved in the activity or issue being addressed. In contrast, individual initiative networks (IINs) are configurations of autonomous individuals and their supporters, usually comprised of volunteers (either self-selected or recruited by the network leader).

With appropriate training and direction, GIGs have proven useful for incremental organizational improvement. They have also demonstrated significant limitations, particularly if the change required is radical rather than incremental.

However, even when GIGs are given broad charters, have strong encouragement from management, and generate great enthusiasm, their results are frequently disappointing. Often, group members concentrate on their own organizations and specialties and ignore cross-functional interfaces—or they are confused even about where to begin.

One manager of a research-and-development organization that I worked with tells of three separate GIGs, composed of competent engineers and technicians, who were charged with developing recommendations for significant reductions (25 percent or more) in time required for new-product development. The goal, which they set themselves, was recognized as important to business survival. Over the course of several meetings, the following patterns were observed in their interactions:

Issue dispersion. Early discussions ranged over a wide area without focusing on specific issues. When the group was encouraged by both a consultant and its manager to select one or two key approaches, members continued to waver among possibilities. Their eventual result seemed as much an abdication as a recommendation: "Appoint a single project manager with decision-making authority."

Solution dispersion. Group members made few recommendations for major changes in procedures or structures. Those that were proposed received little attention or were side-stepped. Group members were most engaged and talkative when they discussed who could be blamed for existing problems.

Change minimization. After the initial series of meetings, each group was asked to meet on its own to develop specific change recommendations. The quality of recommendations varied among the groups, but even the better ones were limited in scope and would not have resulted in anything near the targeted 25-percent reduction in time.

General-inclusion-group members often approach their tasks with caution. They may be willing to join in discussions that invite them to identify their own problems and solutions rather than having them defined by the manager. But that does not mean that they are ready to explore new horizons. More often, they trudge through familiar terrain after making sure that the trail is safe. Safety frequently involves adherence to informal, perhaps unconscious, guidelines such as the following:

- Avoid threatening others' interests (and they will avoid threatening yours).

- Be careful about making proposals that could affect your job (or the group you represent). You may wind up with more work to do, and management is unlikely to relieve you of any of your present duties.

- Avoid the inevitable risk involved in significant changes.

- Avoid personal discomfort or embarrassment in group discussions; don't depart from group consensus.

- When unsure about what to do, delay by engaging in long discussions of details, semantics, and general principles.

- "Don't fix anything that ain't broke."

The intent of this is to point out the norms, pressures, and inhibitions that affect GIGs. Safety and conservation of the status quo are powerful motivators within most social groups. Well-trained and well-led GIGs have been useful in incremental quality improvement and production problem solving, but even these GIGs tend to produce solutions that are extensions of their current operations, not innovations.

THE INDIVIDUAL INITIATIVE NETWORK

When refinements or improvements of existing procedures are required, trained groups may perform well. However, in today's competitive global environment, improvement of existing procedures may not be sufficient. When new, inventive approaches are required (for example, redefining markets, redesigning structures or major processes), it may be useful to turn again to the vision, initiative, and determination of exceptional individuals, working in voluntary combination to achieve an extraordinary purpose.

As leadership focuses on strategic issues, its perspectives become increasingly abstract. Problems and opportunities appear in the guise of data, trends, policies, and so on. The concept of real people performing their jobs often becomes indistinct and peripheral. However, a thoughtful examination of the day-to-day workings of organizations reveals that, at all levels, important determinants of organizational performance are the thoughts and actions of individual people. Whether it is a chief executive assuming the responsibility for pursuing a new acquisition, a middle manager making a commitment to adopting employee-involvement groups in his or her division, an individual contributor doggedly following through on a technological inspiration, or an hourly employee sacrificing free time in order to qualify for a new job, acts of individual courage count.

> *Inventive approaches call for the initiative of exceptional individuals.*

The individual initiative network (IIN) brings these venturesome people together in voluntary association with others who can contribute to and support their initiatives. The IIN can be a temporary, personally selected advisory group for the CEO. For a middle manager, an IIN may consist of other managers who have similar interests and/or a training specialist, a consultant, and one or two subordinate managers who are enthusiastic about a particular idea—people who want to make it happen. For the individual contributor, an IIN may consist of a few technicians, a marketing specialist, and perhaps his or her own manager. For the hourly employee, the IIN may be a mutual support group of classmates.

The distinguishing characteristics of the IIN include the following:

- An IIN is not usually derived from a typical organization-wide-participation or employee-involvement program. An IIN usually begins organically in response to a problem or opportunity.

- IINs are driven by the individual, often idiosyncratic, visions (sometimes obsessions) of their initiators. These leaders frequently are pathfinders. They are not necessarily popular either within their organizations or among business educators.

- IINs are purpose driven, and their fuel is a mixture of persuasion and power. IINs are usually self-organized, with few of the inhibiting norms of GIGs. Sometimes IINs lack the social sensitivity of GIGs, and this can work against them in the implementation stages of their projects, when the cooperation of nonmembers is required.

- The energy and cohesion of an IIN derives from its purpose, rather than from its relationships. Thus, when the purpose is met, or when it fails, the IIN tends to disband quickly.

What distinguishes the IIN from other groups is the generative, single-minded drive of its leader(s)—and the way in which that drive is transmitted to other members. IIN leaders may not always be the most personable or accommodating people. They may be egocentric, stubborn, and impatient, characteristics that research reveals are common to entrepreneurs. But such single-minded, innovative risk takers have been and continue to be essential to a successful organization.

The drive of the IIN leader is illustrated by the earlier story of the R&D manager who sought to reduce new-product-development time. Disappointed with the lack of substantive recommendations from his three GIGs, but undaunted, the manager personally assumed the responsibility to reduce product-development time by 25 percent or more. After considerable thought and discussion with several of his peers and lower-level engineers and technicians, the manager good-humoredly introduced himself as "cycle time Czar—from product concept to delivery."

From his conversations and from observations at various levels in the manufacturing function, the manager recognized a series of important obstacles in the disparate scheduling systems used by the R&D and manufacturing organizations. In collaboration with the manufacturing manager, he assigned a small group of engineers and technicians to adapt the R&D system to conform with the manufacturing system. This effort clarified several previously unrecognized interface problems and enabled significant corrections to be made.

In its early days, U.S. industry's unique strength was said to have been its "rugged individualism." If we think of individualism as creativity and the courage to venture, it is an exciting prospect.

THE CHALLENGE FOR HRD PROFESSIONALS

HRD professionals have an opportunity to advocate and contribute to the major changes that are required to maintain—and, in some cases, restore— the United States' competitive edge. If these professionals limit their efforts to the encouragement of broad employee involvement in problem solving and other response-oriented activities, they will probably not attain their full potential. An approach that takes into account ways of building on individual strengths is likely to be more productive. Some suggestions for expanding the potential of both GIGs and IINs include the following:

- Recognize the differences between and uses and limitations of individual initiative networks and general inclusion groups.

- Develop "inventories" of specially skilled individuals such as initiators, organizers, and implementers. Assist in building connections between these people and provide training for them in business planning, "political" and group processes, and so on. Encourage them to work in self-organizing teams and provide support.

- Recognize new, continually fluid models of organizational change. Although the classic model of change has been "unfreeze-change-refreeze," our current era may necessitate a new model of "unfreeze-catch the wave-ride it."

- Integrate information and telecommunications technology into OD and training and into thinking about the group work environment.

- Implement approaches to minimize envy, suspicion, and opposition from others toward those who volunteer or are recruited for IINs.

- Train GIG members to avoid "group think," especially in the early stages of exploring issues. (For example, encourage structured debates between those who hold different points of view.)

- Educate employees in constructive followership as well as leadership. Help them to recognize both the values and the pitfalls involved in the consensus-seeking process. Encourage the personal "grounding" and self-esteem required to stand up to prevailing opinion with both civility and conviction during the debate and deliberation phase of decision making and to support decisions once they are made.

- Encourage employees to discover opportunities outside the formal business plan and make things happen outside the formal job description.

Sources of Individual Focus

Carl Rogers, Abraham Maslow, and Fritz Perls were among the seminal contributors to the OD field. The works of all three were predicated on the uniqueness of the individual. They saw each person as a free agent with an inborn tendency to realize his or her own potential. Maslow, in particular, presented a model for the development of the person that included the "peak experience"—an individual encounter with the best within oneself, an opportunity for the person to surpass his or her ordinary level of functioning or perception and reach a new height of performance or insight.

This orientation has declined significantly in the last decade. Even those few current approaches that are focused on the individual are usually "validated" according to statistical distributions from mass testing. A number of current "trait" inventories ask people to answer a series of questions, add up their scores, and consult the table provided in order to find their categories. It is as if we have become more committed to slotting our characteristics into pigeon holes than to exploring the unique aspects of our selves.

We live in an age of demographics. Demographics, the statistical study of tendencies in human population distributions, is a valuable tool for predicting market-segment reactions. Nonetheless, we must remind ourselves that market segments are convenient abstractions, and if the manager (or the HRD professional) forgets to "walk among them," individual people may be reduced to depersonalized units. Perhaps this depersonalization is one cause of the serious problems of stress, substance abuse, and depression found in our society.

Good products are made of good parts. Better communities, better teams, and better coalitions can be built if they are built of confident, competent, and congruent individuals.

As we have discussed, refocusing on individuals is neither easy nor very fashionable at present. In a backlash to the 1960s, the last two decades were times of concentration on systems, cultures, and other large-scale abstractions. Comfort, acceptance, and support can be derived from group affiliation. Identity, freedom, personal strength, and self-realization must all be discovered on one's own.

Stanley M. Herman consults to senior and middle managers in areas of organizational effectiveness such as team effectiveness, implementation planning, individual counseling, and designing and facilitating large-scale organizational change. He has served as director of HRD for major corporations and as instructor at a number of universities and professional development programs. Stan's columns appear in newspapers and magazines; he has appeared in management films and videos; and he is the author of several books, most recently A Force of Ones—Reclaiming Individual Power in a Time of Teams, Work Groups and Other Crowds *and* The Tao at Work: On Leading and Following, *both published by Jossey-Bass in 1994.*

THE FLEXIBLE CAREER:
RIDING THE CAREER WAVES OF THE NINETIES

Caela Farren

Abstract: Surfing can be a metaphor for the work world of today. Today's workers need new and flexible approaches to riding the work waves. Work waters are becoming more and more turbulent for those who are operating out of the old pictures of success. Navigating the new waters of global business requires the perspective, maneuverability, energy, durability, stamina, and zest of surfers. The basic principles that all surfers follow to master the ocean waves offer clues for how to be successful, confident, and competent workers in the 1990s.

People with broad vision who scan vast horizons of industry trends, organization trends, and work trends will be more buoyant than people with limited vision who are dependent on the next raise, the next rung, and the next skill to master. Many former work and career success images now generate failure. New work success maps are needed that will orient workers about the gear, preparation, exercises, companions, equipment, and qualifications needed.

In this article, the author illustrates how navigating the winds of change requires finding balance, seeing patterns, choosing environments, learning to specialize, staying connected, making changes, and discovering passion. With such skills, surfers and workers succeed, regardless of the waves they encounter.

Work and play are two cornerstones of human life. Surfing merges the two in an almost seamless, exciting, challenging rewarding experience. Career success today calls for riding the work waves with the expert skill of a surfer. One must see the approaching waves and possess the agility to change direction quickly and reposition oneself while holding a steady course. Skilled work surfers accept the waves of change as a given. They do not fight the industry or economic change waves; instead, they watch them diligently and plot appropriate courses of action. Rather than wasting time commiserating about the past or present, they look to patterns in the work system to direct their day-to-day learning. They know how to read the tides, ride the crests, choose the waves that fit their levels of competence, and surf with people on whom they can count for learning and support.

FINDING BALANCE

What could be more turbulent, more changing, more exciting, and more unpredictable than the changing tides and currents of the ocean? Surfers search for waves, whitecaps, foam, and tubes; they match the turbulence and excitement of the pounding waves with their well-honed skill and agility. They demonstrate a flexibility that captures observers' respect and enthusiasm. Day after day they ride the waves. They demonstrate the harmony that can exist between the relentless power of the ocean and the personal power, determination, and flexibility of surfers. This temporary, always-sought-after balance (harmony) between the ever-changing waves and the wave riders is the best possible metaphor for demonstrating a worker's delicate balancing act with the ever-changing workplace waves.

Workers today feel shaky. They encounter unpredictability at every turn of the work world—technology, downsizing, acquisitions, alliances, demographic shifts, closings, and regulations. The workplace offers no steady state, no rest, no predictability, and little or no security. Some workers thrive on this uproar; they look ahead, keep learning, keep searching, keep seeing new opportunities, predict changes, and so on. Others are surprised, thrown off guard, outplaced, underutilized, or insecure about the future; they often experience unrecoverable wipeouts.

SEEING PATTERNS

For the untrained eye of the superficial, craftless worker, the work world seems totally out of control. Like unskilled surfers, these workers cannot read the patterns in the waves, cannot scan the horizon for the "right" waves to ride, have not chosen the best surfing companions, or do not have teachers; they topple easily, sometimes forever. They do not foresee plant closings, changes in office technology, the flattening of middle-management layers, the need for increased specialization, or the ebb and flow in market conditions. They do not know what jobs to take, what organizations to join, what parts of the country to locate in, or what crafts, trades, or professions in which to develop skills. They are at the mercy of the turbulent workplace oceans.

Those with trained eyes, who have made a serious study of reading work waves, have fewer spills, fewer short rides, fewer lost surfboards, and many exciting, thrilling, and challenging rides. These flexible workers match their mettle against the speed and power of the ocean.

Although the wave world is out of the surfer's control, many changes can be anticipated by watching the waves and feeling the wind. Skilled surfers (flexible careerists) see the big picture—what is coming, where it is moving, and when it is coming. Futurists spend their time watching and gathering the work trends, and they anticipate the possible results of various waves on the world of work. These future-gazers watch the intersection of various currents (economic, government, technology, global interests, and so on) and how they position themselves to bash industries, demolish companies, or wipe out jobs. They study patterns in the waves with enough distance and perspective and in enough segments of the work world to make very accurate assumptions.

> *Flexible careerists, like skilled surfers, see the big picture.*

So, too, skilled surfers have the broad perspective. The ocean is always changing, moving, and in transition. The waves lap the shores and appear random; yet there is a pattern and predictability in the tides, the hurricanes, the size of waves, and so on. Watching for only a minute or hour in time, a person can see no predictability, no pattern, no clear direction. But students of the wave begin to have confidence in the ocean. They know how to time themselves and become more skilled at predicting changes as they pick up the subtle nuances of the wind and water. They become less scared of changes, for they begin to be forewarned.

Surfers love and accept the changing quality of the ocean. They can even become hypnotized and calmed by the very inevitability of the change. Flexible workers also can learn to read and ride the work waves. They can begin to trust that motion will continue and tides will come in; they begin to pace and time their comings and goings to fit the waves, the tides, the storms, and so on. They move respectfully from apprehension to appreciation, from fear to freedom, from caution to confidence. They ride the waves and give in to their changing shapes. Awkwardness gives rise to awe. Perspective and power come from looking at the broadest horizon and reading the patterns in order to choose the best wave possible for their current skills and abilities.

CHOOSING ENVIRONMENTS

Work and careers are not only about people and their jobs. Work life unfolds in interrelated systems that are constantly changing and influencing future choices. Imagine five concentric circles, pulsating with life and energy, bombarded by waves of change from inside and outside. When one ring of the circle changes form, the others also change because they are part of a single system, like waves in an ocean.

Learning to read the waves is simply a matter of paying attention to the whole system. The world of work (Figure 1) has five rings: the industry, the organization, the profession or field, the work/job, and self. Like waves in the ocean, each of these five work waves are constantly in motion. However, by learning to see the patterns and trends in the waves and by positioning themselves accordingly, smart workers can plan for the longest, most exciting ride possible.

The first step is for people to identify the industry that they are in and the major technical changes and trends that have affected that industry in the past few years. Who are the leaders in that industry? Which companies, individuals, and countries predominate? How are they addressing the technical, economic, and social changes in the industry? These are critical areas for colleagues to discuss if they are to ride the waves of industry changes. The trends in an industry are observable in trade publications, newsletters, company slogans or advertising campaigns, computer bulletin boards, and in discussions with colleagues, clients, strategic planners, and managers. It is difficult for people to design smart careers if they are not cognizant of the change waves in motion and the options they unleash.

Second, people must examine their own organizations or companies. What social, technological or economic waves are hitting—higher labor costs, shorter product-life cycles, new alliances and partnerships, increased teamwork, global markets? Any one of these waves could force workers to acquire new skills, develop teams, learn new languages, or change dreams. Clues about direction and learning abound in company newsletters, job posting boards, technology choices, strategic business plans, and company missions. As directors of their own work destinies, people have to read between the lines and speculate about the impact changes in the organization will have on their career choices. They need to ask the kinds of questions that shed light on new company directions and learn what it will take to stay on top of the waves rather than be caught in the currents.

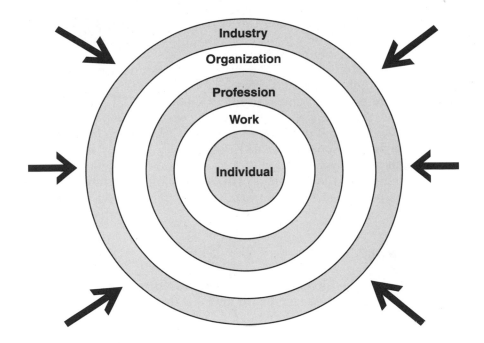

Figure 1. The World of Work

LEARNING TO SPECIALIZE

Some surfers ride the big waves at Sunset Beach while others specialize in the tubes of the Banzai Pipeline. Like the ocean waves, work fields and trades are constantly changing as a result of technology, economic factors, globalization, and changing business directions. Choosing and developing a craft, trade, or work specialty is critical for riding the work waves of the future.

Therefore, the third step is for people to study their business professions or specialties. Too many people concentrate on their jobs and lose track of how their professions are evolving; they then are surprised to find themselves obsolete. A profession is an area of specialization with clear boundaries, recognized experts, and a set of practices and principles requiring mastery in order to be a qualified practitioner. Examples are engineering, finance, marketing, nursing, education, architecture, or accounting. Early in their careers, it is important for people to explore several areas of work. However, eventually they must choose one profession in which to specialize and develop a sense of personal mastery and competency. Some people stay in the same field for a lifetime, and others have careers that span several different fields. What is critical is to choose a profession, study the trends and evolution of that profession, and commit to staying current.

Professions cross industrial and organization boundaries. People need to know whether their professions are primary or secondary to the mission of a particular organization. People working in secondary professions are more at risk and can find their work contracted out or given to temporaries. Because of this, they need to be aware of the major changes in their professions over the past three to five years. They need to identify the experts in the profession and what they are saying about new directions and new expertise requirements in the field. This information contains important clues to maintaining career flexibility.

STAYING CONNECTED

The best surfers have both built their own surfboards and purchased or used state-of-the-art surfboards. As surfboard masters, they always seek to redesign their equipment to give them a new edge or advantage over the ocean power.

Surfers also observe other surfers. They watch how they paddle out to the big waves, how they gaze, their subtle moves on the board, their preparations for springing onto the board, the curve of their backs while surfing the tubes, and myriad other moves that make the difference between wave riders and wipeouts. Surfers are always refining their techniques to have the perfect ride.

In contrast, consider the plight of the average worker. Jobs are designed to meet the mission of the organization and the needs of its customers. Work is bundled into discrete jobs, projects, or work processes. This is a convenient way of dividing the tasks that need to be accomplished on a day-to-day basis. Certain jobs are unique to an industry (such as stockbrokers), while others cross industry lines (such as managers). Jobs come and go at an increasingly rapid pace. Thousands of jobs will emerge this year that were unknown last year. Thousands of jobs will disappear this year, never to be seen again. People who equate their careers to their jobs often experience anxiety and insecurity. They know their jobs are changing and could even disappear. Increased work power is the result of careful answers to the following questions:

- How has this work/job changed in the last year?
- What changes are anticipated in the future?
- What new skills will be needed for success?

- How can more value be added for customers?
- How could work be redesigned or changed to be more productive or more effective?

MAKING CHANGES

Individual needs are changing; moving, marriage, divorce, children, health, leisure, time, financial status, and family pressures all contribute to changing needs. Given these changes, certain companies or industries may be more appealing than others. Being more available for a teenager may require reducing travel time. Taking care of sick parents may require working from home. The more people can anticipate the changes in their personal lives, the more they can tailor their work situations to meet their own needs as well as those of the company.

DISCOVERING PASSION

Surfers have been around for hundreds of years, engaged in the eternal struggle of man against the elements. A sense of harmony and timelessness exists when the surfer, the ocean, the equipment, the wind, the sand or coral underneath become temporarily bonded in the act of "riding the waves." This ride parallels the desires people have to be captivated by work—so drawn into it that they will push all limits to reexperience a sense of accomplishment, union, and personal fulfillment. Nothing is more exciting for the surfer than riding the waves. Nothing is more exciting for today's worker than riding the work waves with confidence, competence, and alignment.

Surfers choose ocean conditions that meet their needs for excitement and safety. Workers need to choose industries and organizations that provide the same. Surfers choose companions who can challenge them, teach them, and support them. Workers need to choose organizations that fit their needs for learning, support, risk, and reward. Surfers read the waves and move in the direction of challenge or security. Workers need to read the patterns of change and determine new skills and competencies required for success. Successful careerists assess the trends in a given company and seek out projects and positions that enable them to take maximum advantage of the waves of change.

Caela Farren, Ph.D., *is an organization development consultant with more than twenty-five years of experience, specializing in strategic business management, organization design, and career and management development. Her clients have included AT&T, Merrill Lynch, Ethicon, Marriott, Bell Labs, Glaxo, Warner Lambert, BASF, CIA, and the Department of Commerce. She is currently CEO of Farren Associates and a principal in Career Systems, Inc., as well as serving as a visiting professor at The American University. Dr. Farren is a member of the OD Network, The American Society for Training and Development, and The Human Resource Planning Society. She is the author of numerous articles and a book,* Designing Career Development Systems.

MOTIVATION IN WORK SETTINGS TODAY: A REDUCTIONIST APPROACH

Thomas H. Patten, Jr.

Abstract: In this article, the author suggests that the traditional theories of motivation (Maslow, McGregor, and Herzberg) may not fit the present generation or the present world. People want more behavioral options and are reluctant to commit themselves to employers or organizations. This article offers a new reductionism that may better fit the motivation of workers in the United States today. This reductionism is more fitting for the contemporary era of greed (1980 to the present) and employment instability.

This article examines existing theories of motivation, relates them to monetary considerations, and suggests reductions that are more applicable in our times. In particular, the concept of fear-greed motivation is discussed.

F or almost thirty years, group facilitators and academicians have used the works of Douglas McGregor (1960), Abraham Maslow (1970), and Frederick Herzberg (1966) as fundamental frames of reference. Although other theories have arisen since then, the popularity of the ideas of these three men has caused a dogmatism in the theoretical standpoints of both facilitators and academics.

However, the present generation in today's world may have different motivational values, which are reflected in employees' behavior. People want more behavioral options and are reluctant to commit themselves to employers or organizations. This article offers a new reductionism that may explain employees' work motivation today better than do Maslow's needs hierarchy, McGregor's Theory X and Theory Y, and Herzberg's intrinsic-extrinsic factors. This reductionism is more fitting for the contemporary era of *greed* (1980 to the present) and employment instability. The previous era, which began in 1950, was one of *need*.

THE DEBATE OVER MOTIVATION

In the past few decades, OD professionals who worked with seasoned managers were often rebuked by those who were skeptical of the ways in which McGregor, Maslow, and Herzberg downplayed the role of money as a motivator. After all, many managers and OD practitioners were continually confronted with employees' demands for pay increases, rate readjustments, a share in business profits, new job evaluations (with the goal of increasing their immediate or potential compensation), and the like. Negative emotions often accompanied these demands by employees, and hard feelings at rejection of their economic aspirations did not die easily (if at all). Inherent job-interest variables and self-actualization seem to be less on the tips of workers' tongues than expectations of annual pay increases and demands for more money. In fact, the desire for more money has created a debate over excessive compensation (Crystal, 1991; Bok, 1993).

In a training or OD setting, the facilitator can manage the climate (if he or she is inclined to) so that critics of McGregor, Maslow, and Herzberg can be appeased or silenced. The participants may superficially tolerate the theory input and dismiss the facilitator as out of touch or naive. Some participants may argue that what McGregor, Maslow, and Herzberg offer is credible. The result may be an intellectual standoff without consensus on the influence of money on the motivation of managers and workers.

A COMMON DENOMINATOR IN MASLOW'S THEORY

Nevertheless, theory input based on McGregor, Herzberg, and Maslow can be useful if it is handled undogmatically. Maslow's ideas are particularly useful for explaining the interrelationships between different types of human needs. Also, it is very easy to point out that all the Maslovian needs can be translated into monetary motives (Patten, 1977).

Physiological Needs

Although the physiological needs are tied to the physical survival of the individual and family, most of these needs can be satisfied by money. If one has the income, one can buy food, clothing, housing, medical care, etc.

Safety Needs

Safety needs are met when protection is provided against danger or threats such as unemployment, discrimination, and favoritism. Economic-security programs and the wherewithal to live in a relatively safe place, travel in a relatively safe manner, hire lawyers to secure justice, and so on, are dependent on money.

Social Needs

Social needs include the individual's desire for friendship, group membership, teamwork, helping and being helped, and the like. They are related to one's reference group—the group with which the individual identifies based on his or her values or social needs—and to belonging and being trusted. Many of the suggested examples of social needs can be satisfied by money, because work for pay helps a person to participate in relatively permanent groups. Money thus brings with it social status and acceptance.

Ego Needs

Ego needs are the needs for self-respect, achievement of status, personal recognition, and the perceived esteem of others. Ego needs also can be met by the mastery of something such as a skill, hobby, job, or managerial role.

Ego needs probably never cease to motivate an individual. In many cultures, money is equated with achievement and is therefore related to an individual's perception of self-worth. Even people who have a great deal of money still seem to want more. These individuals certainly do not need the money for subsistence. For them, making more money than some other person in their reference group is an important achievement.

Need for Self-Actualization

The last Maslovian need is self-fulfillment or self-actualization. This is the need to attain one's potential and be fulfilled in some all-encompassing way. Money alone will not make a person self-actualized, but money will enable many individuals to do what they like with their time and, to some extent, to become what they would like to become. These people have come to the realization that time is probably the most meaningful resource in life; being in control of one's time is an important type of freedom.

Overlapping Levels

Maslow's various needs are interdependent and overlapping, despite the way he delineated them. At any point in time, most people are probably partially satisfied and partially dissatisfied in each class of needs.

Maslow's theory can be applied by managers to life in work organizations, because employees can be viewed individually regarding the level of needs they seem predominately to be on. For example, employees concerned mainly with physiological and safety needs want secure or steady jobs, treatment that gives them preference based on seniority, and a grievance procedure that provides a mechanism for just treatment. These are all they want (if a steady job also means a steady income). They do not want promotions; they do not desire to be challenged or to go higher in the organization.

Knowledge of Maslow's categories can assist managers in understanding much of employee motivation. Of course, if top management attempted to motivate an executive by appealing to him at the physiological or safety level when his prime need was self-actualization, the attempt would fail. On the other hand, any worker would probably be susceptible to such an offer if a reduction in the work force were imminent and that person perceived no equivalent employment alternative elsewhere.

Refinement of Theory Is Needed

Although Maslow's hierarchy of needs may be viewed as a handy managerial tool that makes intuitive sense, it is so general that it needs refinement. It is not necessarily cross-cultural and is more situational than it appears. Most important, as previously indicated, the need levels can be reduced to monetary considerations with little or no stretch of the imagination.

The problem with putting Maslow's hierarchy in this monetary framework is that it would reinforce the widespread prejudgment of some managers that money (one way or another) is the true source of motivation. This conclusion is contrary to Maslow's, McGregor's, and Herzberg's fundamental stance.

Yet many people in the United States today seem to emphasize money and consider other types of motivation at such a low level that what McGregor, Maslow, and Herzberg offered as fresh perspectives many years ago seem no longer to fit (if, indeed, they ever did). Money and materialism—sometimes overlaid with cynicism and blatant self-interest—appear to be the primary motivational dynamics in today's organizations. Perhaps they were always there but were downplayed for ideological reasons in the literature of the social sciences.

It is hard to argue today with young people and young managers about the primacy of money as a motivator. It is difficult to convince them that it is much more (or even equally) important to desire to work under Theory Y conditions, to derive satisfaction in life from intrinsic job satisfaction, and to perform work that has great inherent interest.

> *Pay-for-performance systems are being demanded.*

Nevertheless, they seem to prefer Theory Y to Theory X as the supervisory style under which they work. Also, the circumstances that Likert identified as top-to-bottom, team-built, participative management find wide acceptance (Likert, 1967). Young people seem to expect to have a strong voice in their destinies and work assignments, but money is not demeaned. Performance-based pay increases and on-the-job appraisals of work accomplished (on which pay adjustments and career movements are often based) seem to be getting more attention than ever before.

In trying to discover why pay-for-performance systems are being demanded, we need to turn to different times and places. McGregor formulated his Theory X and Theory Y largely as a consequence of his consulting practices, his World War II experiences as personnel manager at Dewey and Almy Chemical Company, and his unhappy times as president of Antioch College. He apparently learned that from both the individual-motivation and organizational-results points of view, Theory Y (the positive view of human nature) was "better" than Theory X (the negative view of human nature) (Parrington, 1927). Theory Y tied into what Maslow considered the higher order of needs, those that lead to peak experiences and performances and self-actualization. Theory X presumably would never facilitate a person's self-actualization.

Maslow's theory of the hierarchy of needs grew out of a lifetime of work as a clinical psychologist (Maslow, 1968, 1970). His thoughts were widely applied to industrial settings by others. He never considered himself an industrial/organizational psychologist.

When these early applications of behavioral science were made, there was a vacuum in motivational theory. Maslow offered order where there was mostly chaos. Regardless of the validity of the Maslovian theory and its lack of empirical support, many adopted it because it brought together many disparate streams of thought, especially in the field of human-needs theory. Nevertheless, the validity of Maslow's theory has never been proven, if indeed it is even stated in such a way that testable propositions can be set forth to determine the validity of the overall theory.

However, many prefer not to criticize the theory with no equivalent theory to substitute for it, because the void would cause an insurmountable setback. Also, many facilitators and academics hesitate to acknowledge to learners the confusion in the motivational field if they can, instead, present a theory (even an unproven one) clearly and elegantly.

HERZBERG'S THEORY

To his credit, Herzberg (1966) has been an active field researcher and has steadfastly defended his work in front of tough professional audiences. Nevertheless, one may wonder whether the results of studies made years ago in the Cleveland, Ohio, area on several hundred white-collar engineers and accountants should be accepted as true of all workers and, further, whether these results should be reassessed in terms of young people in today's substantially changed work environment.

To be sure, Herzberg's work does not rest solely on those studies, nor should his analyses be cavalierly dismissed as old hat. Nevertheless, his insights into work motivation citing intrinsic factors in the work itself and extrinsic factors in the environment surrounding work need to be reexamined in today's world.

For example, do college graduates in high-tech industries in Southern California have the same motivations as accountants and engineers in Cleveland thirty or thirty-five years ago? Do any of the recent migrants from Mexico, Haiti, or Southeast Asia have the same motivations as those whom Herzberg studied?

Answering these questions requires separating what Herzberg himself might answer (because he is a meticulous researcher) from the typical answers given by group facilitators and academics who offer watered-down theories alleged to be Herzbergian ideas.

The Pay-Administration Variable

There is another facet of Herzberg's work that needs to be addressed. In the last decade, reward systems have been extensively studied by many researchers who look somewhat askance at Herzberg's lack of attention to the manner in which salaries were administered in his study (Lawler, 1990). There is a difference in sound and unsound salary administration that varies importantly by organizational systems experimenting with new pay-plan designs (Schuster & Zingheim, 1992). Today there is more recognition of this important variable.

It is likely that Herzberg ignored the pay-administration variable (the manner in which pay systems work) more than researchers would today. Today the absolute amount of pay is not as important as the way in which pay reflects performance. An adequate system of performance-based pay has hypothetically higher motivational salience than does the traditional pay system in which merit increases are handed out routinely with little or no attempt to differentiate among levels of performance. Interestingly, McGregor (1957) was aware of this and wrote a slightly convoluted piece about it in the *Harvard Business Review.*

THE PERILS OF REDUCTIONISM

To reduce one paradigm to another is detested by some individuals, because in the reduction some richness is lost and the result may appear to be gross oversimplification. Others would argue that out of reductionism comes elegance! Kurt Lewin (1948) is reputed to have been the first to state, "There is nothing so practical as a good theory." We could argue, "There is nothing so practical as an adequate reduction," particularly today, when there is so much verbosity and obfuscation in the management and social science literature.

The crispness of conceptualization of the hierarchy of needs, Theory X and Theory Y, and intrinsic and extrinsic factors was a significant virtue of these theories in their heyday. In a way, these conceptualizations may be perceived as reductions of a hodgepodge of ideas that were floating around shortly after World War II.

Alderfer's Reductionism

Perhaps the earliest and most notable reduction of the big three motivational theories was Alderfer's (1972) reductionism of Maslow into a needs hierarchy of three tiers: existence, relatedness, and growth. This conceptualization did not receive the attention that Maslow received in describing his original hierarchy. However, the logical basis for reducing Maslow's needs to three appears acceptable (Alderfer, 1969).

Existence may have several levels, but they all fulfill the same purpose: survival. Relatedness also can have levels, but the main intention is to tie the person to others. Relatedness would seem rationally to be a compelling need once existence seems assured. The level that enables the person to grow psychologically appears to be salient when the other two have been achieved.

Fear-Greed Reductionism

Another reduction is possible, although the alleged creator of it was not a psychologist but Joseph P. Kennedy, Sr. In discussing Wall Street and the New York Stock Exchange, his words—so the story goes—were something like this: "There are only two emotions that motivate people on Wall Street: fear and greed. All the rest is bull."

Although that comment is amusing, it is worth analyzing seriously, because there is much insight in it. But first let us see where reductionism is taking us (see Figure 1).

Figure 1. Reduction of Maslow's Needs Hierarchy

Samuel Gompers, who was the founding president of the American Federation of Labor (the predecessor of today's AFL-CIO) and other labor leaders of his era told Congress in testimony in the early part of the century that the goal of the U.S. labor movement was more and more and more (Taft, 1949). He is widely regarded as having his hand accurately placed on the pulse of the American worker of his era. Somehow that realization seems to have been denied in the interpretation of early research in the social sciences. But *more* is still the goal of organized labor and, perhaps, of other workers as well.

From 1960 to 1970, one might have received the impression from some scholars that money was a minor matter in industrial employment. They seemed to suggest that employers would be assured of a constant work force on Monday even if they announced on the previous Friday that because the employees' work provided them with inherent interest, and because, on Monday, all employees could plan on having their jobs for the rest of their lives, paychecks would be discontinued on the same day.

The absurdity of this makes a potent point. People need paychecks to provide the wherewithal for living in a modern industrial society. A steady job provides some economic security. A well-paying, secure job can lead to a more secure and gratifying existence. A secure existence reduces fear. The more fear is reduced, the greater is one's feeling of security.

The tendency to want more and more apparently reflects the desire to amass enough money for perfect and total security. In our society, "Don't fool around with my rice bowl" has become "Don't prevent me from obtaining my $350,000 house, Mercedes Benz, trip to Europe, and opportunity to send my son or daughter to an Ivy League college." Self-interest changes gradually to a type of self-centeredness that is raw selfishness.

FEAR-GREED MOTIVATION

The notion of fear and greed can be seen in much that goes on in popular culture and in the literature of the social sciences. In psychology, modern expectancy theory is founded on effort-reward probabilities and mostly self-serving variables (Lawler, 1981). Self-interest is still at the core of economic motivation. Exchange theory in sociology, public-choice theory in political science, and the emerging sociobiology also focus on self-interest. By extension of meaning, the pervasive focus on enlightened or unenlightened self-interest turns out to be supportive of greed.

In a few decades, U.S. workers spurred unions to bargain for more and more and more. Steelworkers were handsomely paid and even given sabbatical leaves if they had long industry service. Labor costs were a primary force that made the U.S. steel industry noncompetitive in the world market (Hoerr, 1988). The pay requirements of auto workers, garment workers, shoe workers, and appliance workers have also knocked down the competitiveness and driven jobs offshore that formerly existed in those industries.

Some companies survived through pay cuts and two-tier wage structures. They got away with these tactics because of increasing fear of unemployment. Yet, in many cases, workers would not accept austerity programs and elected for the company to go out of business rather than depart from the upward wage spiral.

Looking out for oneself has been elevated beyond attention to one's self-interest. One can never be too rich. Jobs in finance and investment banking, junk-bond placement, and corporate takeovers were (and in some instances still are) lucrative career paths that influenced a good share of the best and brightest graduates in the 1980s.

We were told by some politicians that we were entering a "kinder and gentler" era regarding the welfare of all our citizens. However, the aftermath of the 1980s—the recession of the 1990s, the painful and protracted restructuring of the American economy without the weapons and aerospace industry—continues to be an ethos of me-ism and materialism. The plight of homeless people is ignored by large sectors of the population. Tax increases proposed to aid the needy are reviled. Acquisitiveness is accepted as normal at all levels of our society.

Implications for Management

The reductionist theory—which has economic self-interest as its core—can be related to two other concepts that have become popular in recent years in management and OD lit- erature: developing multiple options in managerial decision making and the need for commitment on the part of managers and employees in performing work conscientiously.

> *The reductionist theory has economic self-interest as its core.*

Top-of-the-head problem analysis and snap-judgment decision making are viewed as insufficient and inadequate. Instead proficient managers (so the ideology goes) should create options and analyze problems in depth in order to identify a range of relevant options.

Carried to extremes, identifying multiple options takes a protracted amount of time and may generate so many possibilities that the decision maker decides to delay deciding and "keep all the options open." It is clear that opportunity can become the enemy of commitment and of principled decision making.

Individuals who manage opportunistically form the habit of choosing options that advance their personal self-interests and are personally rewarding. As a result, they do not become committed to the good of the organization. In an environment of downsizing/rightsizing, perhaps this is wise.

The organization and one's position in it are instrumental in determining one's personal rewards and ego satisfaction. If it appears that one's employment is jeopardized, the fear-greed motivation comes into play. One feigns organizational commitment when one needs to. In these uncertain times, work behavior for many people is driven by fear or greed and is essentially opportunistic all the time—devoid of organizational commitment.

CONCLUSION

The need to understand human behavior in organizations causes OD professionals, facilitators, and academics to continue their search for appropriate paradigms. Times change, situations change, and methods of application of theory change. One wonders whether we are ready to adopt a theory to fit the times, situations, and ideologies of today. The fear-greed reduction is as unproven as other theories of the past, but it is as heuristically useful as other theories and it has at least a plausible basis in behavior observed in the United States today. We need to reexamine this reduction and offer it—as well as other theories—to people in group learning experiences, so that they can wrestle with an interpretation that makes sense, is uncomplicated, and fits much of what they perceive better than the Maslovian perspective does.

References

Alderfer, C.P. (1969). An empirical test of a new theory of human needs. *Organizational Behavior and Human Performance, 4,* 142-175.

Alderfer, C.P. (1972). *Existence, relatedness, and growth: Human needs in organizational settings.* New York: Free Press.

Bok, D. (1993). *The cost of talent: How executives and professionals are paid and how it affects America.* New York: Free Press.

Crystal, G.S. (1991). *In search of excess: The overcompensation of American executives.* New York: Norton.

Herzberg, F. (1966). *Work and the nature of man.* Cleveland, OH: World.

Hocrr, J.P. (1988). *And the wolf finally came: The decline of the American steel industry.* Pittsburgh, PA: University of Pittsburgh Press.

Lawler, E.E. (1981). *Pay and organizational effectiveness: A psychological view.* New York: McGraw-Hill.

Lawler, E.E. (1990). *Strategic pay.* San Francisco, CA: Jossey-Bass.

Lewin, K. (1948). *Resolving social conflicts.* New York: Harper & Row.

Likert, P. (1967). *New patterns of management.* New York: McGraw-Hill.

Maslow, A. (1968). *Toward a psychology of being* (2nd ed.). New York: Van Nostrand Reinhold.

Maslow, A. (1970). *Motivation and personality* (2nd ed.). New York: Harper & Row. [Orig. ed., 1954.]

McGregor, D. (1957). An uneasy look at performance appraisals. *Harvard Business Review, 35,* 89-94.

McGregor, D. (1960). *The human side of enterprise.* New York: McGraw-Hill.

Parrington, V.L. (1927). *Main currents in American thought.* New York: Harcourt Brace.

Patten, T.H. (1977). *Pay: Employee compensation and incentive plans.* New York: Free Press.

Schuster, J.R., & Zingheim, P.K. (1992). *The new pay: Linking employee and organizational performance.* Lexington, MA: Lexington.

Taft, P. (1949). *Economics and the problems of labor.* Harrisburg, PA: Stackpole & Heck.

Thomas H. Patten, Jr., Ph.D., *is a professor of management and human resources at California State Polytechnic University—Pomona. He is a well-known expert in such areas as human resource policy, job evaluation, wage and salary administration, performance appraisal, compensation and benefits, organizational development and planned change, and team building. Dr. Patten has also served as a master in chancery and expert witness and consultant in some of the leading pay discrimination cases in the United States. He has written more than two hundred articles and is the author or editor of nine books. In addition, Dr. Patten has consulted with more than fifty companies and agencies in the United States, Western Europe, Canada, Australia, and New Zealand.*

LEADERSHIP STYLES AND THE ENNEAGRAM

Patrick J. Aspell and Dee Dee Aspell

Abstract: The Enneagram is a conceptual framework for understanding human behavior and diversity. Its insights came into use in spirituality and psychology, but have now expanded to be used in human resource development and organizations.

The Enneagram illustrates nine distinct patterns of thinking, feeling, and behaving. By understanding a person's Enneagram, others can better lead, follow, or work with that person. Interactions between people become more successful, and interpersonal stresses are reduced.

The authors describe nine types of leader style and suggest the types of situations in which each style is most appropriate. They then describe the nine types of work styles that one's followers might have and offer suggestions for how best to lead each type of person. Although this article provides only brief snapshots of the Enneagram as it applies to leaders and followers, the system as a whole is a much broader one, with implications for all aspects of human behavior.

The Enneagram (pronounced ANY-a-gram, from a Greek word meaning "nine points," or "nine letters") is emerging on the organizational scene as a valuable tool for human resource development. In 1994, Stanford University hosted the First International Enneagram Conference, which brought together many of the leading authors and contributors. Participants reviewed the Enneagram from various perspectives, and one entire track was devoted to the business perspective.

The Enneagram system is a unique conceptual framework for understanding human behavior and diversity. This system offers such benefits as the following:

- Providing an objective framework of human behavior;

- Recognizing the value of individual differences;

- Identifying strengths and limitations of different leadership styles;

- Being clearly and easily understood;

- Building understanding about various aspects of an organization;

- Helping to assess the fit between a person and his or her leadership position;

- Having profitable applications for areas such as communication, conflict management, motivation, ways of thinking, interpersonal relationships, team building, problem solving, and time management;

- Helping people discover and empower their personality and leadership styles;

- Building a stable framework for emotional issues;

- Helping people be effective with one another in relationships; and

- Enabling people to increase their motivation.

The purpose of this article is to use the Enneagram system to describe nine leadership styles[1] and illustrate how understanding such styles can help in establishing effective leadership.

---

[1] A quick and systematic method of determining a person's leadership style is *The Enneagram Inventory®: Discovering Yourself and Developing Your Style of Leadership, Supervision, and Counseling* (Aspell & Aspell, 1993b).

LEADERSHIP STYLES

Leaders need to manage tasks and lead people according to the demands of the situation; addressing these demands requires answers to the following questions:

- What is to be done? What does the task require?
- Who is involved? Are relationships effective?
- How motivated are employees? Are they proactive and responsible in doing their jobs?

Leaders deal with different situations involving different tasks, different relationships, and different motivations, as illustrated in Figure 1. Each style has certain characteristics and is most appropriate in certain situations.

Leadership Style	What Matters About Tasks?	What Matters in Relationships?	What Is the Underlying Motivation?
1 Stabilizer	Quality	Order	Correct/Right
2 Supporter	Service	Needs	Care/Help
3 Motivator	Efficiency	Doing	Goals/Results
4 Personalist	Creativity	Sensitivity	Uniqueness/Originality
5 Systematizer	Theory	Intelligence	Knowledge/Insight
6 Teamster	Industry	Loyalty	Belongingness/Togetherness
7 Cheerleader	Versatility	Sociability	Satisfaction/Fulfillment
8 Director	Action	Control	Self-Determination/Independence
9 Reconciler	Routine	Harmony	Unity/Peace

Figure 1. Brief Characteristics of Leadership Styles
(Copyright © 1993 by Aspell & Aspell. Used with permission.)

ONE Leaders: Stabilizers

ONE leaders guide people to do what they should do according to principles or regulations. Stabilizers have the following characteristics:

- Following standard operating procedures;
- Insisting on technical competency and skills;
- Requiring quality performance;

- Making sure products and services measure up to clear criteria; and
- Treating people fairly.

This leadership style is most appropriate at the following times:

- When precise, formal policies are to be followed;
- When set cultural norms and values exist;
- With punctual, hard-working employees;
- When thoroughness and attention to detail is demanded; and
- When deadlines must be met.

TWO Leaders: Supporters

TWO leaders encourage people to develop their individual talents in doing a job. Supporters have the following characteristics:

- Recommending help from employee assistance programs and human resources;
- Communicating general expectations in a friendly manner;
- Encouraging people to take initiative in solving problems and planning tasks;
- Assisting people when they are stymied in dealing with a problem; and
- Finding what is best in people and coaching them to grow.

This leadership style is most appropriate at the following times:

- When promoting high levels of customer service is desired;
- In developing participative teams that let all members utilize their skills;
- For monitoring and satisfying the needs of customers and employees;
- In facilitating the development of responsible employees; and
- When training people to appreciate their talents.

THREE Leaders: Motivators

THREE leaders motivate people to take the initiative in achieving positive outcomes. Motivators have the following characteristics:

- Persuading people to work efficiently;
- Communicating with enthusiasm and stimulating employee interest;
- Socializing and talking with employees;

- Pursuing objectives until they are met; and
- Encouraging competition in order to get results.

This leadership style is most appropriate at the following times:

- When employees show maturity in taking initiative;
- When projects need to be pushed, even if it means confronting people with higher authority;
- When decisions are needed in order to put ideas into action quickly;
- When followers want to succeed and advance in their careers; and
- When ideas must be communicated effectively.

FOUR Leaders: Personalists

FOUR leaders allow individuals to express their talents in unique and special projects. Personalists have the following characteristics:

- Offering a broad description of the task and required structure;
- Permitting followers to follow their own imagination and intentions;
- Respecting the special talents of individuals;
- Being concerned about how decisions impact on people's feelings; and
- Inviting new and imaginative approaches to projects.

This leadership style is most appropriate at the following times:

- When exploring alternative ways of solving problems;
- In efforts to humanize the workplace with empathy;
- When appreciating what is personally meaningful to employees;
- When distinctive ways to accomplish a task are desired; and
- When intense emotions need to be handled.

FIVE Leaders: Systematizers

FIVE leaders help individuals to perform tasks by providing the necessary information. Systematizers have the following characteristics:

- Organizing ideas about the nature of tasks;
- Explaining employees' responsibilities;
- Allowing followers to choose how to do their own projects;
- Thinking clearly and logically before making decisions; and

- Keeping emotions under control and the mind focused on problems and solutions.

This leadership style is most appropriate at the following times:

- When planning long-range projects;
- When followers need to be shown a broad view of the purpose of their tasks;
- When certainty is desired before taking action;
- In order to understand what is happening in work situations; and
- When delegating responsibility to employees.

SIX Leaders: Teamsters

SIX leaders promote commitment and cooperation among followers. Teamsters have the following characteristics:

- Seeing themselves and their followers as members of a team;
- Wanting employees to collaborate for the common good;
- Promoting loyalty and dependability among coworkers;
- Relying on team efforts to solve problems; and
- Fostering team thinking.

This leadership style is most appropriate at the following times:

- When following tradition and established ways of proceeding;
- When followers are willing to work hard;
- In order to maintain and/or develop team spirit;
- When a clear chain of command is preferred; and
- When leaders and/or followers possess a high sense of duty and responsibility.

SEVEN Leaders: Cheerleaders

SEVEN leaders foster positive climates for employee satisfaction on the job. Cheerleaders have the following characteristics:

- Motivating employees to be enthused about tasks;
- Encouraging followers to anticipate positive outcomes;
- Boosting morale;
- Planning tasks for satisfactory results; and

- Speaking in a lively way with metaphors and stories.

This leadership style is most appropriate at the following times:

- When brainstorming new ideas and solutions;
- When tackling different or challenging tasks;
- When looking for innovative strategies and practices;
- When there is a need to adapt to changing situations; and
- In order to help employees learn new skills.

EIGHT Leaders: Directors

EIGHT leaders direct followers by ordering them to do the job. Directors have the following characteristics:

- Asserting themselves in the face of challenging projects;
- Being decisive and firm in taking charge;
- Convincing followers in a forceful manner;
- Doing jobs their own way; and
- Deciding independently how jobs are to be done.

This leadership style is most appropriate at the following times:

- In order to stand up under pressure;
- When prompt and tough decisions are needed to complete a project;
- When the leader must be the one to take initiative and perform;
- When training inexperienced workers; and
- When a situation needs to be controlled.

NINE Leaders: Reconcilers

NINE leaders coordinate the activities of people to work together smoothly. Reconcilers have the following characteristics:

- Mediating conflicts among people;
- Negotiating agreement between opposing views;
- Downplaying problems to accommodate people;
- Listening calmly to complaints; and
- Taking time to make decisions.

This leadership style is most appropriate at the following times:

- In order to empower people to get along together;
- When there is a need to be realistic and down-to-earth;
- When doing routine work with set procedures;
- When a unified, harmonious team is desired; and
- When the situation calls for a patient and even-tempered leader.

UNDERSTANDING OTHERS' WORK STYLES

Knowledge of the work styles of others is essential for effective leadership. Without this knowledge, a leader may not understand his or her followers; as a result, he or she may send those followers information in a way that does not make them feel understood, appreciated, respected, acknowledged, or validated. However, with knowledge of his or her followers, a leader can adapt his or her responses, create rapport, and lead the followers to develop their own talents and abilities.

Work Style ONE: Quality Performers

People with this work style work conscientiously to do a job correctly. They are able to stay at one task for a long period of time and dislike being interrupted at work by non-work-related conversation. Preferring to follow operational procedures, they strive to ensure that each particular step in a task be done well. Such people like to be thorough and accurate with the details of a project, taking one step at a time in coming to reasonable conclusions. They are precise in stating facts, and are good at thinking of ways to improve products or services. Quality performers want to treat people fairly.

Work Style TWO: Helpers

Helpers like to be with people in the workplace and show them that they are interested in them. They support others, make them feel welcome in a group, and help them do their work. Such people tend to be sympathetic to—and respond to—the needs of others. Helpers are interested in how decisions and projects affect people. They also like to be thanked.

Work Style THREE: Producers

People with this work style enjoy talking with others about tasks and can motivate them to do their jobs. They work efficiently to get things done and, under pressure, can work to get things done quickly. Goal-oriented people, they want results quickly, communicate by talking about results, and usually pursue goals until they reach them. Producers are good at deciding practical ways to use resources, including people; they can recall peoples' names and use enthusiasm to persuade people.

Work Style FOUR: Expressionists

Expressionists are concerned about the feelings of others and sound them out before acting. However, they prefer inner communication with their own feelings and emotions, even in terms of how they feel about a particular project. Such people can be imaginative in exploring new possibilities and tend to imagine unique ways to get a job done, often taking artistic or aesthetic approaches. People with this work style enjoy acquiring special skills for dealing with unique situations. This means, however, that they dislike doing the same ordinary work over and over and may alternate between enthusiasm and lack of interest for a particular job.

Work Style FIVE: Thinkers

People with this work style are good at analyzing problems, reflecting on the theory behind a project, and exploring the speculative possibilities of theories and ideas. They are satisfied working by themselves, preferring silence in order to concentrate. Consequently, Thinkers dislike being interrupted on the job by phone calls. Although they can apply themselves to a task for a long time, they tend to reflect before taking action, which can lead to their neglecting to act in some cases. Thinkers like acquiring new insights and thinking skills, especially by listening to a tape or reading alone.

Work Style SIX: Relaters

Relaters are cooperative and like to work with reliable people. They are capable of working hard and working consistently on a single task without a break. They tend to prefer communicating within a circle of trustworthy people, people who belong to their own group or organization. Relaters feel most secure working within a group or organization and want to know how the group sees a situation before making decisions. People with this work style like the customary and established ways of doing a job; they get to work on time and keep traditions and/or duties foremost in their minds.

Work Style SEVEN: Animators

People with this work style enjoy a variety of interests and like making people happy. They are interested in innovative ideas and the possibilities of a situation, leading them often to become involved in more than one project. As the name suggests, Animators usually move quickly, sometimes impulsively. They get enthused easily about new projects and tend to be impatient with routine jobs. Because they like to talk with people, Animators like to familiarize themselves with new projects by conversing with others.

Work Style EIGHT: Asserters

Asserters like to take action and be in charge of a project. They can be tough minded and direct, capable of rebuke or reprimand when necessary. People with this work style are willing to take on challenging projects and like to complete the projects they start. They do this by being able to work under pressure, make quick decisions, and convince others to do things their way while rallying them to meet deadlines.

Work Style NINE: Receptionists

People with this work style make people feel at ease. Because of their concern about people working in harmony, they like disagreements to be settled as soon as possible and like to follow previously accepted agreements. Receptionists patiently consider the facts; they want to be calm and collected during each step in a task, calmly reasoning one step at a time to a conclusion. Their desire for people to get along leads them to accommodate others and to get along with many different kinds of people.

EFFECTIVE LEADERSHIP

With knowledge of the follower's work style, a leader can adapt his or her responses by observing the appropriate principle (Figure 2), matching the approach to the particular requirements of a situation, creating rapport, and leading people to develop their talents and abilities.

Leadership that is anchored in principles steers a steady and stable course amid the changing situations of life, work, and relationships. Personal principles (Aspell & Aspell, 1993b) originate from an individual's leadership style and express the values that are important to him or her. The objective application of these principles requires that they be appropriately directed toward an individual's work style in a specific work situation. By following the relevant principle, a leader is more likely to be effective.

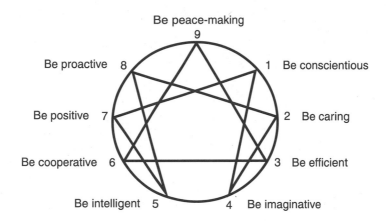

Figure 2. Leadership Principles
(Copyright © 1993 by Aspell & Aspell. Used with permission.)

Leading a Quality Performer (ONE)

Be conscientious. This means living by ethical principles; being competent in performance; thinking reasonably and rationally about problems; being disciplined in pursuing goals; maintaining integrity under pressure; treating others with fairness and objectivity; striving for excellence at work; balancing personal and professional life; and keeping priorities in order.

Leading a Helper (TWO)

Be caring. This means helping others in need; assisting others in solving problems; being of service to customers and clients; giving of time and energy to the organization; being aware of others' feelings; being friendly and warm to coworkers; supporting people in their efforts to grow; expressing appreciation for the work effort of coworkers; and encouraging subordinates to develop their talents.

Leading a Producer (THREE)

Be efficient. This means setting goals to be achieved; defining the mission of the organization; being ambitious in accomplishing objectives; motivating oneself and others to attain goals; communicating effectively to coworkers; calculating and putting in order useful means to reach goals; being practical in working out steps to attain goals; persevering to succeed; and competing with oneself to improve outcomes.

Leading an Expressionist (FOUR)

Be imaginative. This means creating unique products; making service special; being in touch with one's own feelings; finding personal expression in products and services; listening to what others are feeling as well as saying; intuiting original approaches to problems; respecting every person as a unique individual; focusing on what is personally meaningful for each person; and being authentic and true.

Leading a Thinker (FIVE)

Be intelligent. This means being alert and observing products and services; being insightful in work situations; asking relevant questions about the nature and purpose of the organization; breaking down complex problems into simpler ones; anticipating the consequences of policies and strategies; learning thoroughly the organization, people, and products/services; appreciating how others think; keeping in mind a vision of the organization; and grasping the connections between motivation, satisfaction, and productivity.

Leading a Relater (SIX)

Be cooperative. This means bonding with others to work as a team; forming positive personal relationships with others; developing strategies to build trusting relationships; recognizing and accepting the worth of others; developing a mutual support system for coworkers; being committed to the team and organization; developing a sense of belonging among coworkers; being reliable and hard working; and trusting in oneself while depending on others.

Leading an Animator (SEVEN)

Be positive. This means being flexible in adapting to new and changing situations; being proactive and responsive to what is going on in the organization; promoting satisfaction among coworkers; inspiring others with enthusiasm; being adventurous in exploring innovative possibilities; planning for a more enjoyable workplace; generating new concepts and options for meetings; giving others the freedom to grow; and building positive morale among coworkers.

Leading an Asserter (EIGHT)

Be proactive. This means being confident in one's abilities; taking action to complete projects; challenging coworkers to follow through in their commitments to the organization; determining what needs to be done to overcome obstacles; being direct and straightforward with others; being courageous in facing difficult times; arranging to make things happen in a team; using power and authority for constructive purposes; and defending others against unfairness.

Leading a Receptionist (NINE)

Be peace-making. This means being receptive and open to suggestions; being calm and stable during times of disagreement; accepting the diversity of others as positives; listening patiently and gently to grievances of coworkers; respecting different approaches to problems; mediating disagreements among opposing persons or parties; welcoming suggestions about how people can get along together; balancing opposing interests to negotiate equitable settlements; and thinking in terms of a global vision that includes everyone in an organization.

CONCLUSION

The Enneagram theory of leadership is consistent with the right-and-left brain model. On the one side, the left-brain characteristics—analytical, rational, linear thinking—are found mostly in the leadership styles of the methodical One, goal-oriented Three, analytic Five, and dialectical Eight. On the other side, the right-brain features—intuitive, imaginative, spiral thinking—operate usually in the leadership styles of the affective Two, creative Four, inclusive Six, and positive Seven. The corpus callosum, which connects the left and right brains, is represented by the unifying Nine, the harmonizer of opposites.

The full concept of leadership involves both personal, subjective qualities and specific, objective, situational needs. The Enneagram provides a blueprint for an all-encompassing notion of leadership that adapts to the diversity of leaders in the workplace, the variety of followers, and the changing challenges of the marketplace.

References and Bibliography

Aspell, P., & Aspell, D.D. (1992). *Unlimited empowerment: Discovering and enhancing your personal and professional life via the Enneagram.* San Antonio, TX: Lifewings®.

Aspell, P., & Aspell, D.D. (1993a). *Empowering relationships: Discovering and enhancing your personal and interpersonal life via the Enneagram.* San Antonio, TX: Lifewings®.

Aspell, P., & Aspell, D.D. (1993b). *The Enneagram inventory®: Discovering yourself and developing your style of leadership, supervision and counseling.* San Antonio, TX: Lifewings®.

Aspell, P., & Aspell, D.D. (1993c). *The Enneagram inventory®: To discover and develop your personal leadership style.* San Antonio, TX: Lifewings®.

Aspell, P., & Aspell, D.D. (1994). *Chart of the nine Enneagram personality types and professional styles.* San Antonio, TX: Lifewings®.

Aspell, P., & Aspell, D.D. (1994). *The Enneagram inventory®: Building better relationships with people.* San Antonio, TX: Lifewings®.

Aspell, P., & Aspell, D.D. (1994). *The Enneagram inventory®: For career and life management.* San Antonio, TX: Lifewings®.

Aspell, P., & Aspell, D.D. (1994). *The Enneagram inventory®: For creating teams and building teamwork.* San Antonio, TX: Lifewings®.

Aspell, P., & Aspell, D.D. (1994). *The Enneagram inventory®: Styles of communication and effectively influencing people.* San Antonio, TX: Lifewings®.

Aspell, P., & Aspell, D.D. (1994). *The Enneagram inventory®: Styles of conflict management.* San Antonio, TX: Lifewings®.

Aspell, P., & Aspell, D.D. (1994). *The Enneagram inventory®: Styles of thinking and problem-solving.* San Antonio, TX: Lifewings®.

Aspell, P., & Aspell, D.D. (1994). *The Enneagram inventory®: Total quality transformation.* San Antonio, TX: Lifewings®.

Aspell, P., & Aspell, D.D. (1994). *Enneagram workbook for total quality empowerment.* San Antonio, TX: Lifewings®.

Aspell, P., & Aspell, D.D. (1994). *Nine personal leadership principles.* San Antonio, TX: Lifewings®.

Aspell, P., & Aspell, D.D. (1994). *Profiles of the nine personal professional Enneagram styles.* San Antonio, TX: Lifewings®.

Forster, S., & O'Hanrahan, P. (1994). *Understanding personality types in the workplace.* Oakland, CA: Author.

Goldberg, M.J. (1994). The Enneagram: A key to understanding organizational systems. In J.W. Pfeiffer (Ed.), *The 1994 annual: Developing human resources* (pp. 243-255). San Diego, CA: Pfeiffer & Co.

Patrick J. Aspell, Ph.D., *is a licensed professional counselor and an organizational consultant with Aspell Empowerment Enterprises. He presents workshops and seminars to public and private organizations, especially on the applications of the Enneagram to leadership, supervision, team building, career management, and professional development. In addition to numerous articles, Dr. Aspell has coauthored a number of inventories and books applying the Enneagram to business.*

Dee Dee Aspell *is the founder and principal of Aspell Empowerment Enterprises. She presents workshops and seminars, specializing in supervisory/leadership empowerment, team development, and conflict and emotional management, particularly through the use of the Enneagram system. She is the coauthor of a number of inventories and books applying the Enneagram to business.*

SENSITIVE-SUBJECT TRAINING: CONSIDERATIONS FOR TRAINERS

Daphne DePorres

Abstract: Organizations and individuals exist within ever-changing environments. Increasing technological complexity, environmental uncertainty, and the need for adaptability require employees to rely heavily on interpersonal skills and the ability to learn. As they are asked to respond to changes in organizational culture, training in sensitive subjects is often indicated. For the purposes of this article, sensitive-subject training is training that requires participants to examine their assumptions and their behaviors. Examples of sensitive-subject training include diversity, conflict resolution, mediation and communication skills.

Sensitive-subject training calls for more considerations on the part of the trainer than less emotionally engaging subjects. By being aware of the challenges of sensitive-subject training, the trainer and developers of training can design and deliver training that will be successful in achieving the organization's objectives, foster productive relationships among organizational members, and truly engage the participants in the training.

As an organization responds to its environment, training is often indicated. When the required shift involves changing or reinforcing the values, assumptions, or beliefs of the human beings that populate the organization—the very culture of the organization, the training can be termed "sensitive."

For the purposes of this article, sensitive-subject training is training that takes place within an organizational context and requires participants to examine their assumptions and their behaviors. Examples of sensitive-subject training include diversity, conflict resolution, mediation skills, and communication skills.

Sensitive subjects may not be seen as sensitive to participants when they voluntarily attend training, have asked for training, or are participants in sessions where they have anonymity. This article focuses on training in which attendance is mandatory, participants have little desire for such training, and participants attend training with their work groups or other organizational members. Trainers of sensitive subjects often face groups that are far more reserved and resistant than "ordinary" training groups.

Sensitive-subject training calls for more considerations on the part of the trainer than less emotionally engaging subjects. By being aware of the challenges of sensitive-subject training, the trainer and developers of training can design and deliver training that will be successful in achieving the organization's objectives, foster productive relationships among organizational members, and truly engage the participants in the training.

WHO ARE YOU AND WHERE ARE YOU?

Trainers can begin by looking at their own experiences. A person of color who has faced discrimination, a woman who has been sexually harassed, a middle-aged white male who has been laid off, a parent who has been refused family leave, a gay or lesbian who has been threatened with bodily harm, a manager who has seen many programs come and go, or an employee whose boss has had a grudge against him or her from day one—all of these people have work to do before they train in a sensitive subject.

Trainers cannot bring significant unresolved emotional issues into the training room. These issues will show through any veneer, unconsciously affecting training. Trainers with unresolved issues who must do sensitive-subject training might seek the confidential counsel of a respected and trusted colleague. When delivering sensitive-subject training, it is helpful to have colleagues with whom to consult about issues and challenges that arise during training.

Is It Safe Here?

The role of a sensitive-subject trainer requires much more than sharing information and guiding participant learning. For information and learning to be received, it is critical that the environment allows participants to feel safe enough and comfortable enough to participate.

The participants themselves should help in developing the ground rules for the training, the temporary norms that will shape an environment conducive to sensitive-subject training. This can be done simply by asking the participants the question "What are the conditions you'd like to have present in order for you to participate fully in the training?" Typical responses include honesty, open-mindedness, full participation, respect for others, and confidentiality. By establishing their own ground rules, the participants are more likely to take ownership for the environment in which the training takes place.

Confidentiality

Participants often bristle at a request for confidentiality, knowing that an agreement in that area will likely be broken. Indeed, much of the participants' internalization of sensitive-subject training occurs after such a training, when they discuss and debate the issues among themselves.

What many participants assume is that the request for confidentiality means that nothing that occurs in the training should be repeated outside of the training. It is important to clarify agreeing to confidentiality means that agreeing not to repeat what other participants have said and done. Participants are always free to share their own thoughts and perceptions of the training with others. They are always free to repeat what they themselves have said. Clarifying what confidentiality means often relieves this anxiety.

Group Size

Participant involvement and participant safety are also dependent on group size. Clients and trainers must seriously consider the objectives of the training and how much change is expected when determining the size of the training group. If the sensitive-subject training is expected to shift an organization's culture, it is critical to engage the participants in the learning. One trainer in a group of ninety participants is unlikely to engage the whole group or even a significant portion of it. The situation is compounded by the fact that often participants in a sensitive-subject training do not want to be there. The probability of deep and lasting results can be increased by carefully considering group size. In general, the depth and scope of the expected results are inversely proportional to the size of the training group. For a sensitive-subject training that is expected to contribute significantly to organizational change, the training group size is best set at between fifteen and twenty-five (Zander, 1989).

> *...the depth of results is inversely proportional to the size of the group.*

Previous participants of sensitive-subject training report that smaller group size encourages the committed exploration of sensitive subjects. Participants in small groups more willingly participate in exercises and engage in dialogue. In contrast, participants in larger groups report feeling "on display."

Setting

With sensitive-subject training, it is important to maximize the connections between participants, provide space for movement, and minimize distractions. Trainers and participants typically are accustomed to classroom-style arrangements with hefty manuals and workbooks poised on tables draped with hotel linen. Technical training may rely heavily on such things in order to be successful, but sensitive-subject training usually concerns human beings in relationship with one another. Therefore, it calls for a different way of looking at supporting materials and room arrangements.

Circular and U-shaped seating with tables removed may feel threatening to participants, and they often do not appreciate it at first. However, the primary motive of such settings is to remove as many barriers to participation and learning as possible. This means minimizing the use of manuals, videos, tables, overheads, and other typical accoutrements of learning. Although this may seem radical, examining assumptions and subsequent behavior changes require an environment where exploration, experimentation, and practice are encouraged.

Participation

Sensitive-subject training often accomplishes more than the sharing of information and the development of skills. Team building is often a byproduct of experiences in which participants have opportunities to communicate at deeper levels.

In sensitive-subject training, the subject matter requires that participants trust one another, that problem solving occur in a supportive atmosphere, and that the group learn the value of "constructive conformity" (Dyer, 1987, pp. 15-16).

Sensitive-subject training attracts a lot of attention, especially when the first sessions are taking place. Sometimes managers or the human resources department ask to have observers present. It is advisable to be very cautious about having "previewers" in the training sessions. If it is absolutely necessary to have a visitor in the training, that person should take part in the training as a participant. And, depending on the identity of the visitor, it may not be possible to avoid inhibiting the group.

The Presence of the Leader

Leaders sometimes feel that they inhibit participants and wonder whether or not they should attend. This is a legitimate concern. In the training room, assumptions about leaders may result in participants' trying to please, not speaking freely, being judgmental, being argumentative, and any number of other behaviors. Leaders may become the focus of participant ill will, derailing the real learnings desired during the sensitive-subject training. However, inasmuch as sensitive-subject training typically includes an examination of assumptions, it is appropriate to discuss assumptions about leaders as well as those about groups.

Setting the Tone

Setting the tone for the training right away clarifies the level and type of participation expected during the sensitive-subject training. Introducing a nonthreatening and interactive activity as soon as possible also helps participants quickly move through the discomfort of having been summoned to sensitive-subject training. In addition, involvement and activity also diffuse the challengers, those participants who have been waiting to disrupt or discredit the training, declare it to be nonsense, get the trainer on the defensive, or question the trainer's credibility.

In the opening moments of the training, participants are likely to be reserved, resistant, detached, or hostile because they are wondering what could be so wrong with them that they need fixing. Participants are concerned about being confronted, blamed, shamed, and exposed before their peers and colleagues. By setting the tone early on, the trainer can help the participants to relax and be ready to take part.

Language and Vocabulary

Trainers of sensitive subjects have become accustomed to the language associated with these subjects. However, participants, waiting to be attacked, often react very strongly to words such as racist, prejudice, confrontation, bias, and so on.

Purists will argue that when talking about a subject, the most commonly used language is the language to use. What trainers need to consider is whether or not the language commonly associated with the sensitive subject creates a safe environment for exploration, inquiry, and positive change. Using language that puts participants on the defensive will prevent or seriously delay the advent of learning. Participants begin with deeply ingrained assumptions about words as well as groups. For example, often when trainers substitute the word "filters" for "stereotypes," participants demonstrate a willingness to get involved and explore the stereotypes they have associated with groups and individuals. Use of alternative words does not mean avoiding real issues and delicate subjects; however, it allows the trainer to consider to the desired outcomes.

> *The language used needs to create a safe environment for exploration.*

Other Considerations

Sharing personal experiences. Trainers need the confidence to share how their own behaviors have gotten in the way of learning and effectiveness.

Having fun. Sensitive-subject training can and should be fun. Although the subject is serious, feedback for sensitive- subject training clearly indicates that participants remember more and internalize more when they have had fun.

Skill building. Sensitive-subject trainers often have only one opportunity for the training, and time is always short. A simple way to reawaken the latent skills most participants already possess is to provide an opportunity for skill practice. A case study tailored to the particular organization can provide an opportunity for participants to practice conflict resolution, effective communication skills, and apply learnings about the subject. Trainers also can incorporate into the skill practice an opportunity for participants to list and record the skills that help them to be effective. Common skills mentioned are listening to others, paraphrasing what is said, trying to understand the other person's point of view, using "I" instead of "You" language, avoiding defensiveness, and so on.

CONCLUSION

By carefully considering the dynamics present in any sensitive-subject training, the trainer can increase the odds that the organization and the participants will learn. The trainer can also transform the sensitive-subject training from being emotionally and physically draining to an enjoyable and rewarding experience.

References

Dyer, W.G. (1987). *Team building: Issues and alternatives* (2nd ed.). Reading, MA: Addison-Wesley.

Zander, A. (1989). *Making groups effective.* San Francisco, CA: Jossey-Bass.

Daphne DePorres is the executive director of the St. Martin Institute, a management consulting firm specializing in organization development. Areas of specialized experience include conflict resolution, effective communication skills development, understanding and managing diversity, anti-racism training, executive development, small-group process effectiveness/process consultation, and personal development and effectiveness. Additionally, she has more than a decade of managerial experience in Quality Assurance and technical staffing with a Fortune 500 consumer products company. Recent clients include General Mills, Inc.; Grand Metropolitan-Pillsbury; Dayton Hudson Corporation; Northern States Power; United Way of Minneapolis; St. Croix Valley Memorial Hospital; and the Minnesota Council on Foundations.

CREATING AND MOTIVATING EFFECTIVE TEAMS: THE CHALLENGE

William A. Snow

Abstract: Although the concept of teams is not new, the process of shaping effective organizational teams is still evolutionary. Team members and leaders need to understand the dynamics, issues, and challenges of this form of accomplishing work. This article briefly summarizes the stages of team development and the team issues and behaviors that occur in each. It then discusses the elements of team effectiveness: goals, roles, procedures, and interpersonal functioning. Finally, it discusses the relationships between team effectiveness and training, decision making, the knowledge worker, job security, equitable rewards, and continuous improvement.

O ne organizational response to our era of rapid change and increased competition has been the creation of various types of work teams: high performance teams, self-managed teams, and cross-functional teams. Presumably this organizational form offers its members more autonomy, empowerment, self-direction, and job satisfaction.

Teams are groups of two or more people who must coordinate their efforts in order to accomplish a task. If a job can be done by one person, using a team is a waste of resources. However, when a task requires several resources, a well-functioning team is the most effective way to complete it.

As executives become more aware of the positive correlation between teamwork and organizational performance, their need increases for more knowledge about team development and about the factors that contribute to and detract from team effectiveness.

TEAM DEVELOPMENT

One key to building effective teams is understanding the stages of team development that occur over time. Some models by well-known researchers (Bennis & Shepard, 1956; Gibb, 1964; Moosebruker, 1987) contain four stages of team development; others contain five (Drexler, Sibbet, & Forrester 1988; Tuckman & Jensen, 1977). These stages can be summarized as follows:

- Stage 1: Creation
- Stage 2: Conflict
- Stage 3: Cohesion
- Stage 4: Contribution
- Stage 5: Recreation

Creation. During the first stage, team members move from an individual to a team orientation. Team tasks include identifying behaviors that are acceptable to the team and team members' skills and agendas. A leader typically is selected, and his or her role is to provide structure and reduce ambiguity in the team.

Conflict. In stage two, the central concern is developing trust and collaboration. Conflicts tend to arise as members express needs for power and achievement. Leadership may change. Individuals may believe that their needs can be better met through their own actions than through the team.

Cohesion. There are two primary foci of stage three: solidification of members' roles and the quality of the team's decision-making process. Team norms are developed mutually. By now a team personality has been established, and the benefits of team effort are apparent.

Contribution. Teams in stage four are mature; they possess confidence in their abilities, willingness to confront both interpersonal and task issues, involvement, motivation to contribute, acceptance of responsibility, active participation, and productivity.

Recreation. When the team's membership changes, the team needs to reform. When the team's task ends, the team needs to disband. If the team is to end, the members need to take time to acknowledge team achievements and participate in some termination ceremony.

The developmental nature of these stages requires that the activities of each be accomplished and the problems of each be resolved before the team can move to the next stage. Major issues in each stage are of two types: task (work activity) and interpersonal (member behaviors).

Figure 1 displays team-effectiveness issues that typically surface in each stage of team development.

TEAM EFFECTIVENESS

As teams form, they need to pay attention to their processes as well as to procedures that help them function effectively. Effective teamwork does not happen naturally; it takes practice.

Many issues create potential problems for teams. These issues need to be resolved in a hierarchical manner. Therefore, a team needs to address first its goals, then its roles, then its procedures, and then how its members function interpersonally.

Goals

The effective coordination of a team's resources rests, in part, on the ability to specify the objectives the team is attempting to achieve. Conflict can be expected around how much time and energy should be allocated to various tasks because of different perceptions of the team's mission or goals. Much energy is wasted if objectives are not understood and agreed to and if priorities are not established. The latter is particularly important, because it directly affects how choices and decisions are made.

Stage of Development	Stage Indicators	Task Activities	Team-Member Behaviors	Issues
One: Creation	Newly formed team New department or supervisor Many new team members New project/product/service Major reorganization	Developing mission Initial action planning Establishing accountability	Introductions Communications from leader Low risk taking	Empowerment Communication Work force diversity
Two: Conflict	In-fighting in team Team members taking sides in arguments Task assignments not completed on time Others taking control from formal leader Competition among group members Confusion on assignments and tasks Some members totally withdrawn	Clarifying roles Establishing measures Defining goals	Power struggles Polarized arguments Various conflicts	Communication Teamwork Trust Balance Role clarity
Three: Cohesion	"Family" attitude prevails Candid, two-way communication People involved in the workplace Work considered "fun"	Tackling assignments Generating data Reaching consensus on goals	Input of ideas by all Trust built Communication open	Balance Accountability Decision making Teamwork
Four: Contribution	Major milestones and deadlines reached Presentations made on outcomes Collaboration and participation when warranted High quality/high output	Reaching major milestones Solving problems Continuous improvement	High level of commitment Candid interplay High trust levels	Communication Teamwork Balance Accountability
Five: Recreation	Major projects accomplished, team in maintenance mode Initial plan worked to completion Major organizational change, focus, or realignment Team and individuals rewarded for accomplishments	Accomplishing initial plans Process maintenance Planning for next steps	Victory celebration Sense of accomplishment Rewards and recognition	Empowerment Work force diversity Accountability Teamwork

Figure 1. Team Task Activities and Member Behaviors

Pfeiffer & Company

Roles

The next set of problems is related to roles. Ambiguities in "who should be doing what" can only be partially handled by formal job descriptions. Job descriptions should not be relied on to cover the day-to-day contingencies that arise when an interdisciplinary team attempts to accomplish a task.

Many problems arise simply because team members are not clear about what they expect of one another. A person may be silent in a team meeting because he or she thinks the purpose of the meeting is educational (someone is teaching something) rather than problem solving (everyone is here to contribute).

Often, much energy is wasted because team members do not know the procedures to develop clear role definitions. Three types of role conflicts frequently arise. The expectations that others have of a team member can be in conflict with the person's personal expectations. The expectations that two or more team members have of another person can be incompatible. Finally, the total expectations held of one team member may require more time and energy than the person has in a workday.

Procedures

The focus of goals is "what"; the focus of roles is "who"; and the focus of procedures is "how." Procedures are mechanisms for sharing information or making decisions and protocols to facilitate coordinated activity. Effective teamwork requires clear, agreed-on procedures in the following areas:

- How decisions will be made,
- How conflicts/problems will be resolved,
- How often team meetings will be held,
- Who will attend, and
- How team meetings will be conducted.

In some team settings, the answers to such questions are specified in advance. In other settings, the answers are developed by the team members.

Interpersonal Functioning

Whenever team members work closely together to achieve a task, they develop feelings about one another. The extent to which team members respect, trust, support, and feel comfortable with one another influences how they work together.

The consequences of negative feelings are clear in the team members' behaviors. They avoid one another, snipe at one another (directly or indirectly), and find working together to be difficult.

The interpersonal issues of a team also affect the goals, roles, and procedures. Therefore, team members need to decide how they are going to function interpersonally and commit to operating within those agreed-on boundaries. Because of the developmental nature of teams, periodic reassessment of this element is essential.

Goals, roles, procedures, and interpersonal functioning are basic elements of team effectiveness. Effective resolution of issues related to these elements is essential in improving teamwork. Solutions to team problems are based, in part, on understanding which elements (goals, roles, procedures, or interpersonal functioning) the problems are related to.

THE CHALLENGE OF TEAMS

As organizations have attempted to become more efficient, many have turned to the creation of teams—self-managed teams, high-performance teams, cross-functional teams, and so on. Many such efforts have not been successful, despite the well-intentioned efforts of organizational leaders and followers. Much of this dilemma can be explained in terms of some basic realities regarding team motivation and performance.

Reality 1: Teams Need Proper Training

In order for teams to function effectively, they must be trained to do so. Such training includes making decisions about goals, roles, procedures, and interpersonal functioning. Periodically asking the question "What keeps us from being as effective as we might be?" strengthens the team and keeps it on target. Team members may need training in communication skills, problem identification, decision making, and other skills. An integral part of team training is an understanding of how teams develop and the issues they face in each stage of development.

Reality 2: Teamwork Takes Time

Kanter (1983) discusses the dilemmas of participation. Teams generally take time to plan, implement, and follow-up on their work because input from team members is vital to the output that is desired. There is a tradeoff. If an organization wants quick turnaround, it may decide to forego the participation, commitment to the work, quality, and increased morale that well-trained teams (particularly self-managed teams) can produce.

Reality 3: The Knowledge Employee Is Different from the Production Employee

The move from an industrial to a post-industrial society has occurred in a relatively short period of time. The world is now in the information age. Workers involved in the actual production of goods constitute fewer than 9 percent of all workers (Naisbitt & Auburdene, 1985); the great majority of the work force is doing something else. That something else involves inputting, processing, interpreting, and using information. The knowledge worker is an integral component of the information age. Such workers want challenging and interesting work; a satisfactory work environment; positive working relationships; more control over planning and decision making related to their jobs; and more participative leadership styles.

Reality 4: Employees Are Concerned About Job Security

Until recently, loyal and hard-working employees had high job security in most organizations. A major change in organizational life includes the need to be more competitive in the global economy. Many organizations have attempted to achieve this by "downsizing" (or "rightsizing") and restructuring. Often such attempts create a lack of job security that impairs employee motivation and productivity on a continuing basis.

Reality 5: A Revolution in Employee Rewards Is in Progress

When teams are formed as a result of downsizing or restructuring, the members—as survivors—are typically delegated additional work responsibilities. All too often, commensurate adjustments in compensation do not follow. Sometimes, the message seems to be that the survivors should be grateful that they still have jobs. Over time, however, people expect to be rewarded equitably for their contributions.

The revolution in employee rewards centers around the concept of rewarding employees based on their output. The reasoning is that rewards should be based on the value added by the employee. Thus, it is entirely possible that an employee might not receive any adjustment in her or his compensation until there has been value added (productivity) by that person. A variety of variable-output reward schemes operationalize this idea.

Reality 6: Continuous Improvement Is Central to Customer Satisfaction

The harsh reality is that in order for organizations to be competitive and cost effective, they must deliver consistently high-quality services and products to their customers. Global competition is forcing the issue of quality. Thus, the question is not whether to integrate quality-improvement principles into an organization but how to begin the process.

One aspect of quality improvement that tends to be neglected is improving services to internal customers. Internal quality control and improvement is fundamental to providing a quality product or service to external customers. This necessitates that departments and work teams view their fellow employees as customers. Work teams need to discuss quality issues that are a result of one group's output being transferred to another work group (their input). If quality is to improve, interactions within the organization must improve.

Team functioning is effective when leaders and team members understand the stages of team development; have the proper training to engage in teamwork; have clear, agreed-on team goals, roles, and procedures; have interpersonal skills; and face the organizational realities that accompany the use of work teams.

References

Bennis, W.G., & Shepard, H.A. (1956). A theory of group development. *Human Relations, 9*, 415-437.

Drexler, A.B., Sibbet, D., & Forrester, R.T. (1988). The team performance model. In W.B. Reddy & K. Jamison (Eds.), *Team building: Blueprints for productivity and satisfaction* (pages 45-61). Alexandria, VA: NTL Institute, San Diego, CA: Pfeiffer & Company.

Gibb, J.R. (1964). Climate for trust formation. In L.P. Bradford, J.R. Gibb, & K.D. Benne (Eds.), *T-group theory and laboratory method: Innovation in re-education*. New York: John Wiley.

Kanter, R. (1983). *The change masters*. New York: Simon & Schuster.

Moosebruker, J.B. (1987). Using a stage theory model to understand and manage transitions in group dynamics. In W.B. Reddy & C.C. Henderson, Jr. (Eds.), *Training theory and practice* (pages 83-92). Alexandria, VA: NTL Institute.

Naisbitt, J., & Auburdene, P. (1985). *Reinventing the corporation*. New York: Warner.

Tuckman, P.W., & Jensen, M.A.C. (1977, December). State of small group development revisited. *Group and Organization Studies, 2*(4), 419-427.

William A. Snow, Ph.D., *is a professor of organizational psychology in the organizational psychology department at the California School of Professional Psychology. He consults internationally with a variety of public and private sector organizations, especially with CEOs and top management in the areas of team and organization effectiveness, rewards, and strategic planning. He is a member of the Education Roundtable of the National Management Association for whom he authored* Leadership in the New Era, Organizing and Leading Work Groups, *and co-authored* Business Ethics, *(with Tom Von der Embse), and* Managing Change *(with Paul Clipp).*

APPLYING BUSINESS PROCESS IMPROVEMENT TO A TRAINING DEPARTMENT

Beverly Ann Scott

Abstract: Business process management and improvement concepts were applied to the development of a business-unit training department to be integrated into a corporate-wide organization and management development function. A corporate program in business process improvement was developed on the basis of the department's effort to align values, strategies, and organizational needs.

Core activities of the training department were identified, and a model of core processes was developed. Process "owners" and project leaders play key roles. Continual review of processes facilitates continual learning and improvement.

Business process improvement (also called business process reengineering) is the "hot" intervention in organizations today. One of the reasons is that, if done properly and thoroughly, it works. In order to obtain the desired results, organizations must understand and integrate certain basic concepts. These are as follows:

Employees are empowered to respond to customer needs. This concept emphasizes the value of employees who are able to respond promptly to customer requests without going upward in the hierarchy to obtain information, approval, or authority. Staff members should be trained and empowered to respond to clients in the most appropriate manner and to utilize the resources of other staff members as needed.

Flatter, more efficient organizations are created. Employees empowered with the information, skills, and authority to plan and monitor their own work and address customer needs need fewer supervisors and managers to watch over them, organize and direct their tasks, or intercede with customers.

Organizations are customer driven. Decisions and actions need to be evaluated in terms of the needs and requirements of customers.

There is a focus on process. A process is a series of activities; there is a specific input, something is done to it to add value to it, and the result is an output to an internal or external customer. Almost any activities in business can be defined in terms of processes. For example, core processes in a training department include consultation, design of programs, and delivery of programs.

People own their processes. Owning a process contrasts with managing a function, which tends to create boundaries without concern about how activities flow and integrate to meet customer requirements. Owning a process involves a new set of responsibilities: understanding the customer's requirements, paying attention to the flow of activities and how well one activity is integrated with the next, monitoring quality and efficiency, and working to continually improve the process.

People work in cross-functional teams. Team members who share expertise and resources across functions ensure integrated activities. All members are accountable for outcomes that meet customer requirements.

There is an emphasis on business process improvement. This may refer to improvement in parts of processes or to total process redesign, which may involve radical change.

A Case Study

In the process of integrating a new training department into an existing, for corporate-wide organizational and management development function, we decided to use the concepts of business process improvement. The rationale was that if we applied these concepts within the department, we could better communicate them to and implement them in the larger organization.

Core Goals and Values

One of our core goals was to create a learning organization in which open communication and training would facilitate continual improvement and skilled, empowered, customer-focused employees and teams. We based our goals on the following set of values:

- Trust and respect for one another and for our customers.
- Care to balance the needs of individuals, relationships, and the organization as a whole.
- Continuation of our own growth and development in order to be able to provide the resources and solutions needed by our customers.
- Valuing of our differences and sharing of ideas and resources in order to collaboratively produce better products and services for our customers, both individually and in teams.
- The provision of competent, consistent, high-quality work.
- The maintenance of confidentiality.
- Empowerment of team members to meet mutually agreed on goals and responsibilities.

Strategy

We developed a strategy to achieve our goals, based on the following tactics:

- Integrate training and development into the company's overall business strategy.
- Consult with corporate management and business-unit management about organizational redesign, restructuring, and realignment.
- Design, create, and deliver learning and development opportunities that support business strategies (e.g., alternative delivery technologies and customized training modules).

- Transfer the skills of consultation, facilitation, and training by providing training of trainers, coaching, and shadow consulting.

- Integrate skill development into larger organization development efforts.

- Continue to improve programs and processes with current technology and trends.

- Define processes and standards that ensure quality.

Application

Although the department's goals, values, and strategy, and the concepts of business process improvement were the bases for applying process improvement to our department, we also developed an organizational rationale for our recommendations:

- To utilize resources more effectively and efficiently to meet organizational needs.

- To provide a consistent management of quality and responsiveness to customer needs.

- To provide opportunities for development and to provide daily coaching of all levels of staff.

- To develop integrated and coordinated approaches to both individual and organizational learning.

We developed a model of our core processes (Figure 1). The input of customer needs and business strategy feeds the core processes of design, training delivery, organization development, and management development. In the center, strategy and concept development integrate these processes. Surrounding all these are support and client and project management. The output is individual and organizational learning. Figure 2 lists the activities included in each process.

Next, we defined process owners and project leaders, diagramed the structures (see Figure 3), and described accountability.

A process owner is responsible for:

- Ensuring efficiency, quality, and customer responsiveness;

- Developing and coaching other staff members whose time is allocated to that process; and

- Coordinating and integrating with other processes.

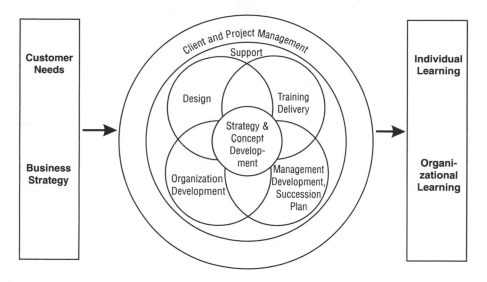

Figure 1. Model of Training Department Processes

Design

- Needs analysis and diagnosis;
- Classroom, self-study, multimedia, and just-in-time (JIT) training;
- Format for delivery;
- Technical, skills, sales, supervisory, and management training;
- Evaluation.

Training Delivery

- Employee, sales, supervisory, and management training;
- Coaching and training trainers from line management and HR;
- Coaching and development of HR staff training skills;
- Optional delivery systems;
- Evaluation.

Organization Development

- Needs analysis and diagnosis;

Figure 2. Activities in Training Department Processes

- Line and HR management consultation on organizational change;
- Facilitation of business process improvement, problem solving, planning teams, and task forces;
- Team development;
- Survey-feedback development;
- Evaluation.

Management Development and Succession Planning

- Succession-planning process;
- High potential/executive development;
- Development planning;
- Consulting and coaching managers on subordinate and own development;
- Assessment processes and tools;
- Identification of external resources for development;
- Coordination of library resources;
- Educational assistance.

Strategy and Concept Development

- Strategy formation to support business strategy;
- Integration of models and concepts across processes and programs;
- Development of models to meet client needs;
- Application of new technology, methodology and models.

Support

- Logistics coordination;
- Production;
- Publishing;
- Clerical and administrative support.

Client and Project Management

- Planning, coordination, and implementation.
- Project management;
- Customer interface.

Figure 2 (continued). Activities in Training Department Processes

Training Department Management

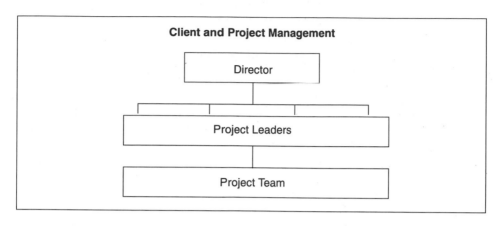

Client and Project Management

- Director
- Project Leaders
- Project Team

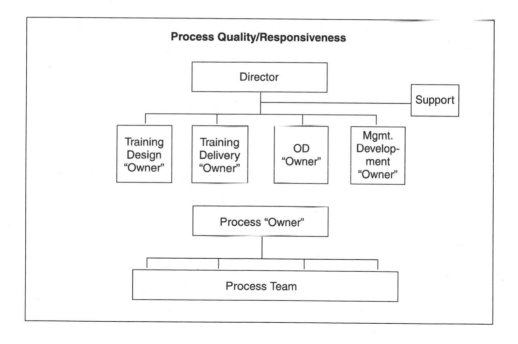

Process Quality/Responsiveness

- Director
- Support
- Training Design "Owner"
- Training Delivery "Owner"
- OD "Owner"
- Mgmt. Development "Owner"
- Process "Owner"
- Process Team

Figure 3. Training Department Structures

A project leader is assigned to coordinate and manage a project and is responsible for:

- Managing a project team composed of members from appropriate processes (e.g., design, delivery, consultation);
- Customer interface and satisfaction; and
- Meeting project deliverables and outcomes.

Implementation

As we created our new department, we found continuous learning and continuous improvement to be key guiding principles. For example, the design-process owner has developed tools and processes to increase the quality and efficiency of the design process. We have created an improvement team to review our evaluation proccsses and to recommend improvements and higher level evaluation. As we have learned more about our processes, we have designed the flow of our macroprocesses with more detail, as is shown in Figure 4.

Finally, we continue to examine our goals and our vision of our future. The use of business-process improvement concepts continues to be a useful and practical approach to our work.

Beverly Ann Scott is director of organization/management development and training for McKesson Corporation. She is responsible for the corporate and operating-unit management, organization development, and training efforts. Before joining McKesson, she was a development consultant for the Bendix Corporation and an external consultant. Her interests include large-systems change, management development, and human resource strategy. Ms. Scott coauthored Quality Circles, *published in 1982, and she has published articles in industry trade journals about change and employee involvement. For five years, she also served as editor-in-chief of "Vision/Action," the professional journal of the Bay Area Organization Development Network.*

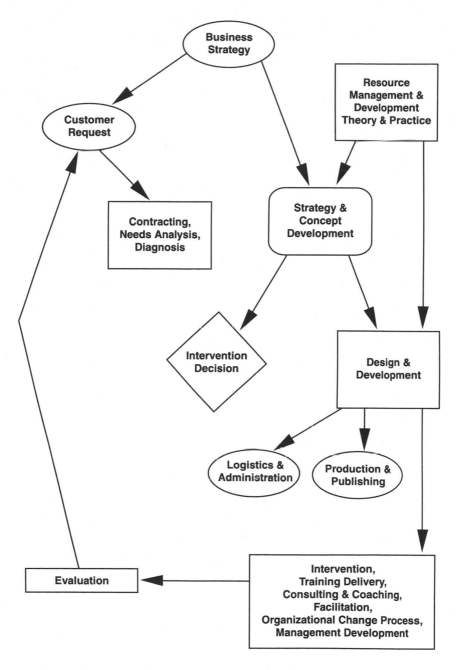

Figure 4. Flow of Training Department Macroprocesses

Understanding Change
From the Gestalt Perspective

Hank Karp

Abstract: Change is inevitable, and it is inherently neither good nor bad. People can handle change in one
of three ways: (1) the "traditional" approach (desiring
no change), (2) the "dynamic" approach (desiring
constant change), or (3) the "pragmatic" approach
(desiring productive change).

Productive change requires two phases: presenting
the change and working with the resistance. The
change leader must work with both phases and provide a process that will facilitate a specific change
easily and effectively with minimum disruption and
maximum support from the group. The four basic
styles of change leadership (autocratic, participative,
supportive, and laissez-faire) each have appropriate
applications, depending on the particular circumstances. However, the change leader's most important
function is to help people to understand that they
have the skills needed to implement positive change
and that they are already using these skills effectively
in their personal and professional lives.

Most people perceive change as disruptive and to be avoided whenever possible. The paradox is that the only thing that is constant and that we can depend on is that change will occur. In fact, adapting to change is something that we all do all the time. We may not even notice it unless attention is called to it.

In thinking about change, we need to recognize that change is neither good nor bad, it just is. The key is to recognize that change is neutral, that it occurs, and that it is perceived as good or bad depending on the conditions.

THE CHANGE CONTINUUM

One way to envision change is as a continuum. All human characteristics and capacities are polarities, e.g., good-bad, strong-weak, tall-short, and so forth. The capacity for change also can be viewed as a polarity. On the far left of the continuum is "no change" (e.g., life in a Trappist monastery); on the far right of the continuum is "constant change" (e.g., an Army recruit's first two weeks in basic training).

No Change	Productive Change	Constant Change
Traditional	Pragmatic	Dynamic
Past	Present	Future
Change Is Bad	Change Is Inevitable	Change Is Good
Values What Was	Values What Is	Values What Might Be
Older	Wide Range	Younger
Resists Change	Honors Resistance	Suppresses Resistance
Stagnation	Growth and Effectiveness	Chaos

Figure 1. The Change Continuum

The Traditional Approach

In the illustration, the left polarity describes the condition of no change. This typically is described as a "traditional" approach. A person who wants no change is focused on the past, probably conservative in terms of values, and perceives almost any change as a threat to the established order. The position is that if something is new, it is bad. Traditionalists who are key policy makers and people of influence tend to be in their mid-fifties and early sixties. At dinner, they compare the meal to the best one they had ever had. Although the traditionalist position does provide stability, comfort, and minimum threat, it also carries the seeds of boredom, lack of opportunity, no growth, and increasing levels of individual and interpersonal stagnation.

The Dynamic Approach

The right polarity describes the condition of "constant change." This can be referred to as a "dynamic" approach. This position is focused on the future. The position is that if something is new, it is good. Any change is seen as positive, and any resistance to change is seen as behind the times. People who hold the dynamic view who are key decision makers and people of influence tend to be in their thirties or early forties. At dinner, they think about what they are going to have for breakfast. Although the dynamic position does provide energy, excitement, and activity, it also produces a great deal of motion without meaning, mindless jargon, the tendency toward surface treatments, and a growing inability to focus on what is really important. The move is toward chaos.

In their rush to leave the traditional ways behind, many of today's organizations have charged into a set of dynamic organizational norms and values and are not much better off for having made the switch.

The Pragmatic Approach

The third position, in the center of the continuum, is the condition of "productive change," which can be described as the "pragmatic" approach. This position is focused on what is happening now and is characterized by flexibility. Change is perceived as inevitable; however, how one responds to it is a matter of conscious choice, even when the choice is for the status quo. Pragmatic policy makers and people of influence tend to span the age range. At dinner, they enjoy the meal.

There is a paradox in productive change: one changes by not changing. That is, when one focuses on what is happening right now, the increased awareness resulting from that focus is a change. How one chooses to respond to the new condition is a matter of conscious choice. It is best determined by considering what is wanted and what is available and then considering the current conditions that are supporting and/or blocking the change. The move is toward growth and effectiveness. It is this position that results in the smoothest transition from one state to the next.

TWO ASPECTS OF THE CHANGE PROCESS

Initiating change is a two-phase process. Phase one is "Presenting the Change," and phase two is "Working with the Resistance" that accompanies almost every change. Most people do a good job in phase one and then stop, not even realizing that phase two exists and that the job is only half done.

In the change continuum, each of the three positions has its own unique response to resistance, just as it has to change. The "No Change" position tends to resist change without thinking because it perceives change as being bad. The "Constant Change" position tends to suppress resistance because it sees change as being inherently good simply because it is. The "Productive Change" position honors resistance because it accepts it as something to be worked with, a natural part of the change process.

EIGHT ASSUMPTIONS

The Productive Change process relies on the following eight assumptions:

1. Change is best facilitated by developing ownership in the change process.
2. Change will occur most easily in an atmosphere of enlightened self-interest.
3. People do not resist change; they resist pain or the threat of it.
4. People tend to resist the opposite of change, which is boredom.
5. Power is the ability to get what you want; resistance is the ability to avoid what you do not want. Resistance is a subset of power, not of change.
6. Resistance is best dealt with by honoring it, rather than suppressing, avoiding, or minimizing it.
7. People can best work with resistance from others by first understanding and accepting their own.
8. Change leadership involves helping people to make better choices in light of current realities and then assisting them in taking full responsibility for making these choices happen.

THE CHANGE LEADER

In working with change, the leader is the person who wants the change to happen and is in a position to work with the group to make it happen.

The role of the change leader is to provide a process that will facilitate a specific change easily and effectively with minimum disruption and maximum support from the group.

The change leader is usually—but not always—the manager or supervisor of the group that has to deal with the change. A group member can initiate and implement a change (e.g., an idea for changing a specific work procedure), as can a quality-improvement team or a human resources representative, just to name a few.

FOUR BASIC STYLES OF CHANGE LEADERSHIP

Despite common myths, there is no one best style of change leadership. Many "experts" advocate a participative or democratic leadership style. This style may be the most effective approach in a majority of cases, but it is by no means the only appropriate style for effectively managing change.

Leadership can be defined as the ability to obtain willing compliance in accomplishing something. In other words, the more you can facilitate a person's performing a task without resenting having to do it or resenting you for having assigned it, the better the leader you are in that situation. Obviously, at some times it is easier to be a good leader than at other times.

As we all know, situations, conditions, and people are constantly changing. To manage change successfully, one must stay flexible and able to respond to what is going on. The more the change is described as what is presently happening—rather than as what should be happening or what might happen next—the easier it will be to work with people in facilitating the change.

Every change leader has a unique style. Each person's style is made up of some combination of the four prototype styles: autocratic, participative, supportive, and laissez-faire. The styles of change leadership are intended to manage change; they are compatible with, but somewhat different from, the standard leadership styles for managing work. What works best for one person is probably that person's primary style, but each change leader should learn to use the other three styles as backup styles (i.e., to be versatile) because different circumstances may call for different styles.

Autocratic

The autocratic change leader makes the demand and the group is expected to respond.

Best When: The demand is simple and there is little or no interest on the part of the group *or* when the demand is externally imposed and not negotiable.

Application: Autocracy is an effective approach to managing change when the change is not important to anyone. Autocracy saves time and reduces resistance to the change, because at least under these circumstances, people are not having their time wasted. *Example:* Determining what the new color will be in all the rest rooms in the building.

> *Every change leader has a unique style.*

Autocracy is also the appropriate style to use when the change is externally imposed and there is no opportunity for negotiation. Implying that there is some choice in a change that is already decided on will do nothing but increase employees' frustration with that change. It is better to state what the change will be and then let the employees simply state any dissatisfaction with it, in order to get it out of their systems. *Example:* Enforcing a new policy of "no facial hair" because of possible interference with safety masks.

Participative

The participative change leader is involved with the change and negotiates the change with the group.

Best When: The group's input is needed to maximize the change outcome and/or heavy resistance is anticipated.

Application: The participative style of change leadership is used most frequently because it maximizes both individual input and ownership in the final implementation. Under this style, the change leader and the group work together to make the change happen. It is the style to consider first if there are any negotiable elements in the change and/or there is a high need for input from the group members. *Example:* An employee-involvement team is formed to investigate and recommend an expensive piece of equipment.

The participative approach is also very effective when there is a large amount of resistance to the change. A participative change leader who is skilled in working with resistance can maintain control of the group process; he or she also can facilitate the group's finding ways to work with the elements that are blocking its acceptance of the change. *Example:* A new policy concerning overtime has been mandated, but each department has some choice in how it is to be implemented.

Supportive

The supportive change leader assists the group in developing a process so that it can deal with the change.

Best When: The group is competent to create and/or implement a change but needs the change leader's support in either running its meeting or getting outside assistance.

Application: The supportive style is most appropriate when (1) the group members are highly competent to implement the change, (2) there is high interest and relatively low resistance, and (3) working relationships and trust among the group members are low. The change leader focuses on how the group is working and makes sure that everyone has a chance to speak, that conflict issues are handled reasonably, and that the atmosphere is a relatively safe one in which to work. The change leader does not become involved in making the change happen. *Example:* The work group is relatively new, and the members do not know one another well enough to have developed good communication patterns or a high level of trust.

A second application of the supportive style is when the group requires outside support to make the change happen, and the change leader knows how to get it. *Example:* A department is converting to a new software application, and access to company training resources is needed to facilitate installation of the new program.

Laissez-Faire

The laissez-faire change leader describes the change to be created and/or implemented and then disengages from the group.

Best When: The group is highly competent to respond, and there is little or no resistance to the change. The change leader may have little specific task expertise in comparison with the group.

Application: The hands-off approach to managing change is very effective when the group members are highly task competent and creative, when they have the interpersonal skills to work well together, and when the change is meeting little opposition. In such a case, the change leader presents the change—or the need for change—answers questions, sets boundaries, and then leaves the group to its own devices. *Example:* An effective research and development team is asked to respond quickly to a customer's unavoidable change in job specifications.

Conclusion

Change should be thought of as a normal part of organizational life, rather than as a special situation that requires concern. The change leader's most important function is helping people to understand that they have the skills needed to implement positive change and are already using them effectively in their lives, both at work and at home.

> **Hank Karp, Ph.D.**, *provides training and consulting services, public seminars, and in-house programs through his organization, Personal Growth Systems, in Virginia Beach, Virginia. His specialties are team building, supervisory/leadership development, motivation, conflict management, and working with power and resistance. Dr. Karp's background is in organizational psychology, organization development, human motivation, and Gestalt applications to individual and organizational growth. In addition to many articles, he has written* Personal Power: An Unorthodox Guide to Success *and* Managing Change from the Gestalt Perspective, *published by Pfeiffer & Company in 1995.*

DOING MORE WITH LESS: HOW TO INCREASE PRODUCTIVITY

Stephen R. Grossman

Abstract: When a company downsizes, much concern is directed toward those who are losing their jobs. However, those employees who remain also need concern; they may feel guilty or fearful, or they may lack confidence and motivation.

Companies who have downsized need to find ways to improve employee morale, increase employee focus, and create financial stability in order to maintain productivity and a competitive edge. In this article, the author outlines six steps to address these needs: visualizing the future, eliminating fear as a motivator, supporting employee input, sharing knowledge, rewarding performance, and encouraging employees to read by investing in a speed-reading course.

Employees refer to reductions in personnel as "firing" people, "canning" them, handing them their "walking papers," giving them the "sack," or "kicking" them out on the street. These are ugly terms; therefore, the first act of many companies faced with such a task is to search for a euphemism. Some companies call it "downsizing"; a few call it "rightsizing"; one even referred to it as "decruiting." To stay competitive—or just keep their heads above water—many major business organizations are letting people go. Public attention is focused on the plight of those who lose their jobs, many after long years of service.

However, the effect of massive layoffs can be equally devastating for those who survive the cuts. These are the employees who have just seen their colleagues—people they know are just as talented and hard-working as themselves—lose their jobs. After a moment of initial relief, their reaction to surviving mass layoffs is one of guilt and fear for the future. Their faith and trust in the company are destroyed. Their support group is gone. Their confidence in the future is shattered. Their motivation is wiped out—and yet these are the people whom the company expects to maintain and even increase productivity!

A big problem faced by these organizations is how to revive flagging employee spirits and set out on the road to financial health. Another concern is how management can entice employees to occupy their minds with the task at hand instead of updating their résumés. This paper presents six concrete steps that can speed this process.

1. VISUALIZING THE FUTURE

Any problem can be pinpointed by describing two states: (1) where you are and (2) where you want to be. The problem is the gap between the present and future states that causes discontent or discomfort.

Many organizations solve problems by analyzing the present state, finding the causes of the problem, and attempting to correct them. This method "fixes only what is broken" and is widely considered a common-sense management tool. Unfortunately this algorithm for problem solving does nothing to change employee mind-set.

To change employees' attitudes and restore their sense of empowerment, an organization must concentrate on the future. It must forget the present state—for the moment—and create a vision of the future. This vision is more than a slogan or mission statement. It is a succinct visual image of life without the problem—a picture of the results of solving the problem.

A *process vision* is a results picture that contains certain cues and clues for getting there. Many companies that talk about vision are referring to a *benefit vision*—a document that describes in minute detail the financial and marketing results that accrue from solving the problem. Benefit visions are generally regarded by employees as company hype and setups for placing blame.

A process vision gives the destination and points out the direction, usually by an easy-to-picture metaphor or analogy. One example of a process vision is an athlete's mental rehearsal of a play. Picture a basketball player just prior to making a shot at the basket. The goal is to get the ball through the hoop, and the process vision is embedded in the mind of the athlete. He or she visualizes the shot, from setup to follow-through, in that split second before the shot is made.

Organizations must provide this type of vision for their employees if morale and productivity are expected to increase. Productive employees must know not only where they are going, but how to arrive at that destination.

2. ELIMINATING FEAR AS A MOTIVATOR

Motivation is the most important factor in creating and sustaining peak performance, and fear is a poor motivator. The *type* of motivation desired also distinguishes between the *willing* employee and the *willful* one. Willing employees are extrinsically motivated. They will perform tasks as long as they can see immediate benefits: perks, pay raises, the corner office, or simply hanging on to the job. When faced with serious obstacles, the willing employees wilt, because they do not possess a feeling of ownership of their jobs; they are in the business just for the money.

Willful employees are intrinsically motivated. They feel a personal responsibility for their work that enables them to turn an "impossible" task into a successful project. They are turned on by the jobs they do. This is precisely the type of individuals a company must keep, and this is the type that can be demotivated by fear or by mandated restructuring. A successful company must invite employees to reengineer their jobs—find out what motivates them and what turns them off—then structure the work around these needs.

Studies on the ways highly creative people function show that intrinsic motivation is a common theme (Amabile, 1983; Grossman & King, 1990). Creative problem solving most frequently comes from people who are "turned on" by their work. As a start to reengineering jobs, management might ask employees the following questions:

- To what extent are you excited about the work you do? Why?
- What are the things you value most about work in general? To what extent are they satisfied or missing in your day-to-day activities?
- What are the things you dislike most about what you do? How might you change them and still get the work accomplished?
- When and under what conditions do your best ideas originate? How might we translate those conditions to the working environment?

3. PLAYING THE ANGEL'S ADVOCATE

Once management has invited employees to suggest ways of improving their work, it should not shoot down every proposal as soon as it is offered. *All* new ideas have flaws and drawbacks, and a very human reaction to new ideas is to dismiss them as rapidly as possible. A successful company must make a deliberate management decision to play the "angel's advocate."

This role is played as follows:

- First institute a *search for utility* and visualize how things would look if the idea did work.
- Break the idea down into its component parts, and then test the underlying assumptions.
- Focus on the positive aspects of the new idea.
- Through reshaping and retooling, find ways to make the idea work.

It may be amazing how an easily dismissed idea could be found to contain innovative pathways and solutions if judgment were deferred for a period of serious consideration.

As a side benefit, the angel's advocacy is a gold-plated morale builder. Rather than a faceless entity sitting in judgment, the company transforms its role into that of a co-creator with the employee. Following are some questions that can lead a utility search for new ideas:

- What does the new idea accomplish?
- Under what conditions might there be a maximum payoff?
- What is different about this idea compared to others?
- What specific mechanisms embedded in the idea can be used to accomplish the objective?
- What general principles are at work in this idea?

- What would it take to keep all the usefulness of this idea and modify it to take care of the parts that are problematic?

4. Sharing Knowledge

Employees cannot be empowered if they are kept in the dark. The more they know about what the company is doing and their place in that picture, the more productive and motivated they will be. Keeping information on a need-to-know basis is a sure recipe for employee suspicion, duplication of effort, and plummeting morale.

Keeping employees in the dark is also impossible. As Ben Franklin once said, three people can keep a secret only if two of them are dead. For example, when I was working on developing a major new product for a well-known corporation, we were constantly impressed with the need for secrecy. We were instructed never to talk about what we were doing, not even to our own families, lest word of the new product slip out to our competitors. Then one day I picked up the *Wall Street Journal* and read all about it. One of the executives, who were doing all the warning, simply could not keep from bragging a little at a party.

And finally, employees do not necessarily want to know all the business; they just become nervous when they suspect bad news is being kept from them. In order to stifle some rumors, one East Coast company put all the documentation relating to the company's business in one room. Any employee could go into that room and examine every phase of the business, from boardroom reports to financial statements. The only restriction was that they could not copy or remove any document. The room was mobbed for the first two weeks. After that, hardly anyone went into the room, but the rumor mill died out completely. Just knowing that the information was available was enough.

5. Rewarding Performance

Different types of people need different types of rewards. For some, it is money; for others, peer recognition; for still others, the chance to let their imaginations roam. A good manager will learn which motivators apply to which employees and will make sure that they receive them. People work best when they feel they are appreciated and when they are shown appreciation in the way that will best motivate them. It could be money, but it could also be public recognition of their accomplishments.

6. Investing in a Speed-Reading Course

Even a small investment like a speed-reading course for the employees can reap large rewards. Keeping up with the literature is time consuming but absolutely vital for keeping the competitive edge. Speed reading works. Providing this skill is a minimal investment that nets a state-of-the-art work force. It is also an investment that tells employees that they are included in the organization's future plans.

Moreover, speed reading frees up employees' time to read more *outside* of their fields. Studies of highly creative performance (Grossman, Rodgers, & Moore, 1988) show that the vast majority of creative breakthroughs come from those with both vertical (field-related) and lateral (general-interest) knowledge bases. For example, George DeMaestral conceived of the idea of Velcro after walking across a field and noticing the way cockleburs clung to clothing. Vertical knowledge made the translation from nature to fabric possible, but lateral knowledge from the outside world caused the creative spark to ignite.

> *Speed reading... nets a state-of-the-art work force.*

In other words, if all that employees know are sports scores and the weather, they are not going to be very creative. Management should encourage outside reading; up to 70 percent of the employees' reading should be out of their fields. If they are given the proper tool—a speed-reading course—they can do it.

The biggest mistake that a business can make is to assume that its employees need to increase their creative performance in order to turn the business around. What is needed instead is a shift in attitude by the business's decision makers—a shift from evaluators to creators.

In my fifteen years of consulting to businesses, I am continually amazed at the wealth of new ideas and talent that are stifled by organizational arbitrariness and bureaucracy. In a downsizing environment, these ideas and people need to be nurtured and allowed to flourish. This can happen only if the environment and culture are modified according to the general principles of this article. To use the metaphor of innovation as an explosion of new ideas, technologies, and ways of doing business, an employee can provide an initial spark but the formal culture must provide the fuse and fuel before the final detonation can take place.

References

Amabile, T.M. (1983). *The social psychology of creativity.* New York: Springer-Verlag.

Grossman, S., & King, M.J. (1990). Eagles, otters, and unicorns: An anatomy of innovation. *Journal of Creative Behavior, 24*(2), 75-98.

Grossman, S., Rodgers, B., & Moore, B. (1988). *Innovation Inc.: Unlocking creativity in the workplace.* Plano, TX: Wordware.

Stephen R. Grossman *is President of Double Dominance, Inc., of Maple Shade, New Jersey, a company specializing in the relationship between creativity and technical problem solving. He has taught, trained, and consulted in creativity, problem solving, and corporate innovation for the past decade. Currently he serves on the faculty of the Creative Institute in Buffalo, New York, and on the faculty of the University of Connecticut Graduate Program. Mr. Grossman is a coauthor of* Innovation, Inc.: Unlocking Creativity in the Workplace.

Contributors

Dee Dee Aspell
Principal
Aspell Empowerment Enterprises
4606 Centerview
Suite 155
San Antonio, TX 78228-1203
(210) 734-2381

Patrick Aspell, Ph.D.
Consultant
Aspell Empowerment Enterprises
4606 Centerview
Suite 155
San Antonio, TX 78228-1203
(210) 734-2381

Ellie S. Browner
Assistant Director
Center for Management Development
College of Business Administration
Florida International University
University Park Campus; BA 329B
Miami, FL 33199
(305) 348-4237

Gary Copeland
Consultant
University Associates Consulting &
  Training Services, Inc.
8380 Miramar Mall
Suite 232
San Diego, CA 92121
(619) 552-8901

Ian Croft
6 Vanessa Street
Sunnybank
Brisbane, Queensland 4109
Australia
07-3457232

Daphne DePorres
2616 Townview Avenue NE
St. Anthony, MN 55418
(612) 789-3817

Caela Farren, Ph.D.
President
Career Systems, Inc.
900 James Avenue
Scranton, PA 18510
(800) 283-8839

Peter R. Garber
Manager, Teamwork Development
PPG Industries, Inc.
One PPG Place
Pittsburgh, PA 15272
(412) 434-3417

John G. Geirland, Ph.D.
Management and Organization
  Development Specialist
Geirland & Associates
4335 Beck Avenue
Studio City, CA 91604
(818) 760-4978

Morris Graham, Ph.D.
Professor of Organizational Psychology
Director of Organization Development
  Program
Brigham Young University
55-220 Kulanui Street
Laie, HI 96762
(808) 293-3640

Steve Grossman
President
Double Dominance
411 North Stiles Avenue
Maple Shade, NJ 08052
(609) 779-0702

Sharon L. Harvey
Marketing Information Manager
Incitec Ltd.
Paringa Road
Murarrie
Brisbane, Queensland 4170
Australia
  07-8679300

Stanley M. Herman
Herman Associates, Inc.
25532 Jesmond Dene Road
Escondido, CA 92026
  (619) 480-1628

Bonnie Jameson
Consultant
1024 Underhills Road
Oakland, CA 94610
  (510) 832-2597

H.B. Karp, Ph.D.
Personal Growth Systems
109 82nd Street
Virginia Beach, VA 23451
  (804) 425-8203

Herbert S. Kindler, Ph.D.
Director
Center for Management Effectiveness
P.O. Box 1202
Pacific Palisades, CA 90272
  (310) 459-6052

Chuck Kormanski, Ed.D.
Pennsylvania State University
3000 Ivyside Park
Altoona, PA 16601-3760
  (814) 949-5058

Kathleen Kreis, Ed.D.
Director of English
Buffalo Public Schools
730 City Hall
Buffalo, NY 14202
  (716) 851-3603

Robert William Lucas
Manager, Training
American Automobile Association
1000 AAA Drive
Heathrow, FL 32746-5063
  (407) 444-7520

Marci Maniker-Leiter
Management & Organizational
  Development Consultant
Maniker-Leiter & Associates
2333 Duxbury Circle
Los Angeles, CA 90034-1017
  (310) 559-4056

Lisa Mayocchi
Department of Psychology
The University of Queensland
Brisbane, Queensland 4072
Australia
  07-3656843

Dwight Errol Miller, Ed.D.
Coordinator of Systems Development
Associate Professor of Instructional and
  Information Science
Academic Support, LAS Division
Brigham Young University
Box 1845 BYU-H
Laie, HI 96762
  (808) 293-3856

Michele M. Moomaugh
President
Reid-Moomaugh & Associates
2050 Pacific Beach Drive
Suite 302
San Diego, CA 92109-6686
  (619) 581-2808

Jason Ollander-Krane
Ollander-Krane/Johnson
70 Zoe Street
San Francisco, CA 94106
  (415) 541-0431

Udai Pareek, Ph.D.
Chairman
Scientific Advisory Committee
Indian Institute of Health Management
  Research
1 Prabhu Dayal Marg
Jaipur 302011
India
  91-141-550700
  Fax 91-141-550119

Thomas H. Patten, Jr., Ph.D.
Professor of Management and
  Human Resources
College of Business Administration
California State Polytechnic University
3801 West Temple Avenue
Pomona, CA 91768-4083
  (909) 869-2423

John Powell
Training Specialist
Bayfront Medical Center
701 6th Street South
St. Petersburg, FL 33701
  (813) 893-6910

Robert C. Preziosi, D.P.A.
Associate Dean
Professor of Management Education
Graduate School of Business
Nova Southeastern University
3301 College Avenue
Ft. Lauderdale, FL 33314
  (305) 476-8912

R. Glenn Ray, Ph.D.
Director
Institute of Education & Training
  for Business
Marietta College
215 Fifth Street
Marietta, OH 45750
  (614) 376-4624

Beverly Ann Scott
Director, Organization/Management
  Development and Training
McKesson Corporation
One Post Street
San Francisco, CA 94104-5296
  (415) 983-8300

Debbie Seid
President
Excellence Within
4141 Jutland Drive
Suite 200
San Diego, CA 92117
  (619) 272-5800

William A. Snow, Ph.D.
Professor, Organizational Psychology
California School of
  Professional Psychology
1000 South Fremont Avenue
Alhambra, CA 91803-1360
  (818) 284-2777 x3021

David P. Tulin
c/o ODT, Inc.
P.O. Box 134
Amherst, MA 01004
  (413) 549-1293

Judith F. Vogt, Ph.D.
Associate Professor, Management/
  Organization Studies
Department of Business Administration
Incarnate Word College
4100 Broadway
San Antonio, TX 78230
  (210) 829-6018

Karen L. Williams, Ph.D.
Assistant Professor of
  Information Systems
Division of Accounting &
  Information Systems
College of Business
University of Texas
6900 North Loop 1604 West
San Antonio, TX 78249-0632
  (210) 691-5784

CONTENTS OF THE COMPANION VOLUME, THE 1995 ANNUAL: VOLUME 2, CONSULTING

---

*See Experiential Learning Categories, p. 5, for an explanation of the numbering system.